Modular Learning in Neural Networks

Sixth-Generation Computer Technology Series

Branko Souček, Editor
University of Zagreb

Neural and Massively Parallel Computers: The Sixth Generation
Branko Souček and Marina Souček

Neural and Concurrent Real-Time Systems: The Sixth Generation
Branko Souček

Neural and Intelligent Systems Integration: Fifth and Sixth Generation Integrated Reasoning Information Systems
Branko Souček and the IRIS Group

Dynamic, Genetic, and Chaotic Programming: The Sixth Generation
Branko Souček and the IRIS Group

Fuzzy, Holographic, and Parallel Intelligence: The Sixth Generation Breakthrough
Branko Souček and the IRIS Group

Fast Learning and Invariant Object Recognition: The Sixth Generation Breakthrough
Branko Souček and the IRIS Group

Modular Learning in Neural Networks: A Modularized Approach to Neural Network Classification
Tomas Hrycej

Modular Learning in Neural Networks

A Modularized Approach to Neural Network Classification

TOMAS HRYCEJ

A Wiley-Interscience Publication

JOHN WILEY & SONS, INC.

New York - Chichester - Brisbane - Toronto - Singapore

Library of Congress Cataloging in Publication Data:
Hrycej, Tomas, 1954–
    Modular learning in neural networks: a modularized approach to
  neural network classification/Tomas Hrycej.
        p.   cm.—(Sixth-generation computer technology series)
    Includes index.
    ISBN 0-471-57154-7
    1. Neural networks (Computer science)   I. Title.   II. Series.
QA76.87.H78   1992
006.3'1–dc20   92-2554
                                                              CIP

Printed in the United States of America

10 9 8 7 6 5 4 3 2 1

To Emily, Anita, and Nathalie

CONTENTS

8 Decomposition of the Represented Mapping   165

9 Decomposing the Network to Minimize Interactions   171

10 Modularizing the Application Task   179

11 Decomposing Network Construction into Knowledge-Based and Learning Parts   189

12 Conclusions   215

PREFACE

This book is about *modular learning in artificial neural networks*. Why is this topic important? In the mainstream of neural network research and applications, neural networks are viewed as unstructured black boxes. This view is convenient as long as no problems (e.g., with learning speed or convergence) occur. However, we cannot expect this state to persist if our artificial neural networks grow and our applications become more difficult. The reasons that a modularization of networks and algorithms is desirable can be grouped in the following way:

1. *Engineering aspects.* If learning is viewed as a monolithic black-box task, there are no intermediate solution stages, and the success of each stage cannot be independently verified.

2. *Complexity aspects.* With growing network complexity, scaling and convergence problems of neural network learning arise.

3. *Psychological aspects.* Findings of developmental psychology show the incremental character of human learning, in which the success of each stage is conditioned by successful accomplishment of the preceding stage.

4. *Neurobiological aspects.* The human brain has a complex structure of cooperating modules.

The conceivable approaches to modularization of learning are very diverse. Those discussed in this book include:

1. Decomposition of learning into modules using various learning types (i.e., supervised and unsupervised learning)
2. Decomposition of the mapping to be represented (e.g., to linear and nonlinear parts)
3. Decomposition of the neural network to minimize harmful interactions during learning
4. Decomposition of the application task into subtasks that are learned separately
5. Decomposition into a knowledge-based part and a learning part

Special regard has been given to the fact that linear algorithms such as Hebbian learning are frequently orders of magnitude faster and more reliable than nonlinear algorithms such as the gradient method. This is why as large parts of the learning problem as possible should be solved by linear algorithms. Nonlinear algorithms would then be confined to the inevitable nonlinear hard core of the problem.

In some cases, such as self-organization and network prestructuring, formal analysis has been necessary to develop useful concepts or to prove important properties of network models. Sometimes, formal treatment has been useful for clarifying the *relationship of neural network methods to classical approaches* such as Bayesian classification or principal components analysis. I believe that this relationship is of particular interest for industrial researchers like myself. However, the *primary goal* of this book is to provide *evidence that modular learning* based on some of the approaches presented *is helpful in improving learning performance*. Since the ultimate goal is always to reach better performance for practical classification problems, most of the methods proposed have been tested on two benchmark cases of considerable size and application interest: (1) a medical classification problem of realistic size (7,200 cases of thyroid disorder), and (2) a handwritten-digit classification problem (20,000 cases). Some of the methods proposed led to substantial improvements in solution quality and learning speed (up to 100 times) as well as enhanced robustness with regard to learning control parameters.

I hope that this book will be stimulating both for *scientists* in suggesting yet undiscovered relationships resulting from the integrating view of learning modularization, and for neural network *application engineers*, in showing how neural network technology can be made more controllable by the decomposition of application tasks.

I would like to thank Professor Wolfram Büttner for many helpful remarks concerning related research and some general statements made in this book. I am also greatly indebted to Dr. Dieter Haban for reading the manuscript and polishing my English.

TOMAS HRYCEJ

Modular Learning in Neural Networks

CHAPTER 1 ⸺⸺⸺⸺⸺⸺⸺

Introduction

1.1 MOTIVATION FOR DECOMPOSITION OF LEARNING

Although there have been several proposals for more structured views of neural networks in the past, and a growing number of them at present, the current *mainstream neural network technology and applications* share two limiting characteristics:

1. A neural network is viewed as a black box, whose structure is not explicit. The only conceptual interfaces on which results are observable are the input and output of the network. This is also true for network architectures whose input and output are not assigned to dedicated input or output units, such as nonlayered feedback networks. Input and output are then associated with certain states of the networks, and the sole items of interest are the initial (i.e., input) state and the terminal (i.e., output) state. Information about intermediate states is neither observed nor exploited for evaluation of computational progress.

2. The structure of neural networks is viewed as monolithic. There are no functional or task-specific differentiations.

As an example, we can take the most frequently used model, a layered feedforward network with backpropagation learning algorithm

(Werbos [166]; Rumelhart et al. [139]). Several aspects of this mono-lithic, black-box view can be observed with this network model.

1. Besides the trivial differentiation into input, output, and hid-den units, they all play the same role in neural data processing. There are no subtasks that would be assigned to network parts.
2. The learning algorithm is applied uniformly to all network weights. For each weight, a gradient of the global error func-tion is computed, and the weight is changed proportional to this gradient. There is no differentiation concerning the inter-dependencies between weight changes or the depth to which gradient propagation takes place.
3. All weights in all layers are changed simultaneously. This is another reason why interdependencies cannot be observed and analyzed. Another consequence of this parallelism (regardless of whether genuine or simulated) is that it reduces learning to a single-pass procedure.
4. A consequence of the preceding item is the lack of develop-mental stages, with whose help we would be able to evaluate the partial progress of the solution of the learning task.

This approach is to a certain degree deliberate. It is based on the observation that some large parts of human brain are relatively struc-tureless or, more exactly, that the complexity of their visible structure is substantially lower than that of the tasks they are solving. It is par-ticularly true of the neocortex, to which most human intelligence is attributed. The neocortex is composed of billions of neurons, but these neurons are merely of a few types, and their connections are organized in relatively few schemes or basic circuits (see, e.g., Shep-herd [147]) that are repeated millions of times. It has even always been an explicit ambition of neural network research to find prin-ciples by which complex computations can be performed by a large number of equal, "anonymous," and simple computational units.

Today, we can say that several such powerful principles have been found. Although we cannot claim that our knowledge of these basic principles is complete, we seem to have reached a point at which it may be fruitful to allocate some part of research resources to the problem of how the huge task of cognitive learning can be solved by cooperation of several known principles rather than searching for a single, yet more powerful master principle. This thesis is supported by observations confirming the idea of brain function as consisting of a relatively large number of highly specialized dedicated structures. In some cases, concrete processing sequences of various neural network principles are assumed (e.g., Rolls's model of hippocampus operation [135]).

Under these circumstances it makes sense to investigate for methods of decomposition that would make neural network learning more efficient. In addition to neurobiological arguments, there are important aspects related to engineering, complexity, and developmental psychology. In the following sections we present arguments in favor of such decomposition. Further arguments can be found in the structure of human brain, which is the topic of Chapter 3.

1.1.1 Engineering Aspects

If an industrial application of nontrivial complexity is developed, the development process is usually broken down horizontally (i.e., to relatively independent parallel tasks) and vertically (i.e., to successive development stages). For example, developing a large software application package is decomposed to at least two vertical stages, system analysis and program coding, and to a number of modules (horizontal decomposition), which are independently designed, coded, and tested.

In addition to organization and management aspects, one of the major benefits of this developmental decomposition consists of the possibility of evaluating the success of each partial task independently. For each partial task, a partial success criterion and verification procedure is defined. If the entire application fails to operate correctly, the search for the cause of the failure can, in turn, be decomposed in correspondence with the partial tasks.

The currently widespread black-box view of neural networks is hardly reconcilable with such a development procedure. Its roots seem to be in the fact that distributed representations in neural networks are difficult to assign to any application *concepts*. However, this technical detail does not necessarily imply that independent *subtasks* cannot be implemented by individual subnetworks. The performance of such subnetworks can then be evaluated by individual performance measures. These individual performance measures may be different from the overall performance measure (typically, mean-squared error or misclassification rate). This is exactly what is necessary to make neural network technology acceptable in an industrial engineering environment.

1.1.2 Complexity Aspects

In the present state of neural network technology, the technology seems to be proven to have a large application potential. To date, a considerable number of successful application prototypes have been reported. A common feature of particularly successful applications is that they are based on relatively small networks. The reason for this success seems to be the careful choice of a realistically simple application rather than the computational power of small networks. It can be expected that in a near future, more complex tasks will be tackled by neural networks.

It is natural to expect that the growing complexity of mappings that are materialized by neural network tasks, and growing network size, lead to growing complexity of learning. For arbitrary mappings, learning is known to be NP-complete (Judd [84]). We know that this is not always disastrous. There are many NP-complete practical tasks for which solutions of satisfactory quality are found routinely. It is also clear that human information processing makes use of some methods for coping with NP-completeness. One of the usual approaches to this is certainly decomposing such complex tasks into parts of manageable size.

We can expect that this approach is also applicable to learning. There are at least two ways to benefit from the decomposition of learning:

1. The learning task is decomposed to several relatively independent subtasks each of which can be solved, despite its NP-completeness. The complexity of the overall task is then linear in the number of subtasks. This will not, of course, pass by the NP-completeness of the global task, but there is a high probability of getting good suboptimal global solutions if at least an intuitively good decomposition can be found without excessive computational costs.

2. For an NP-complete learning algorithm we substitute algorithms of less complexity. Such lower-complexity algorithms

are usually subject to applicability limitations, such as the limitation to linear problems. However, using a *sequence* of low-complexity algorithms may substantially extend the scope of problems solvable by them compared with the isolated use of any of these algorithms.

A typical example of the latter approach is linearization of the problem. For some classes of problems, learning linear classifications is a polynomial-time task (Valiant [156]). The algorithms for linear classification are simple and their convergence to a global optimum is guaranteed. On the other hand, the class of problems solvable by linear classifiers (i.e., problems with linearly separable classes) is commonly viewed as being very limited. This is certainly true if linear classifiers are applied directly to raw input data. However, the class of problems solvable by linear classifiers can be extended considerably by combining them with another simple and well-founded learning principle—preprocessing by quantization. In the next chapters, both approaches are pursued: reducing the problem size (Chapter 5) and transforming the problem to one of lower complexity (Chapter 6).

1.1.3 Psychological Aspects

There is a great amount of evidence from developmental psychologists (e.g., Piaget [125, 126]; Piaget and Inhelder [127]) for the hypothesis that human learning is not one-pass learning. Learning can be broken down into several development stages, for which successful accomplishment of each is a necessary condition for the start of the next. For example, Piaget [125] considers the following stages:

1. The period of *sensomotoric intelligence* is characterized by operations based on direct associations between sensory stimuli and motor responses.
2. In the period of *imaginative intelligence*, concrete, unidirectional, imagination-based mental operations are developed.
3. The period of *formal operations* is characterized by a closed system of bidirectional abstract operations.

The abstract operations of the third stage cannot be developed without a cognitive system of concrete imagination-based operations. The same is true for the second and first stages.

There are also typical mental concepts that are necessary elements for the construction of higher concepts. For example, the concept of a permanent object must necessarily be acquired before the concept of causality (Piaget and Inhelder [127]). In turn, the concept of a permanent object has to be preceded by the construction of temporary objects based on a direct sensory experience.

It also seems clear that human learning is not pure supervised learning. Even if we do not consider the question of the presence of a real or internalized teacher, it is obvious that not all human knowledge and skills are learned in a goal-oriented manner. More usual are learning principles that process all sensory inputs, interpret them with help of the things already learned (Piaget's *assimilation principle*), and extract information that is supposed to be useful in the future. At this point, concrete use of this information is not known. So this learning mode is, to a certain degree, unspecific or universal.

Human learning is thus a mixture of two learning types:

1. Unsupervised, unspecific, and undirected learning, or self-organization
2. Supervised, specific, and goal-oriented learning

Unsupervised learning corresponds, on a higher cognitive level, to concept acquisition or learning by discovery. Supervised learning then uses the concepts acquired by unsupervised learning to establish desired associations.

Although this human learning architecture is not a result of a deliberate design, it is certainly very successful. It is capable of solving problems of seemingly arbitrary complexity, although its learning procedures themselves (as far as they are familiar to us) appear to be rather simple, or more accurately, reducible to simple principles such as the Hebbian rule. This contrasts with artificial learning procedures such as the backpropagation algorithm (Werbos [166]; Rumelhart et al. [139]), which are certainly more sophisticated and powerful than the Hebbian rule. But there are also certain costs of this sophistication. The most important ones are low learning speed, unreliable generalization, and sensitivity to control parameter values. In looking for a remedy, several researchers have attempted to find optimal learning parameters (e.g., Kung and Hwang [96]) or to refine the gradient descent method by additional assumptions about the shape of the error function (e.g., the quickprop method of Fahlman [35]). The modularization approach considered here is, without making a claim of detailed biological plausibility, closer to the biological developmental model.

1.2 GOALS OF THIS BOOK

The primary goals of this book are:

- To survey and investigate the possibilities of decomposing learning in neural networks
- To show that the decomposition of learning is helpful in increasing the efficiency of neural networks for some class of tasks
- To provide means for supporting the engineering view of modularization

To reduce the huge scope of this task, a certain degree of focusing is necessary. In the most parts of this book, I have confined myself to the currently most frequent class of applications, *classification*, and on the currently most widespread network architecture, *layered feedforward network*.

Two exceptions to this rule are modularizing principles based on the decomposition of application task (Chapter 10) and the investigation of exploiting explicit knowledge for network topology design (Chapter 11). These exceptions are justified by the fact that both of these topics are of limited interest for classification applications.

Each decomposition principle is evaluated from the engineering viewpoint. In particular, wherever possible, success criteria for those learning subtasks are formulated, to which the global objective (e.g., the misclassification rate for classification problems) is not applicable.

Although the goals of this book are rather pragmatic, a certain amount of theoretical developments has proven to be necessary. A primary decision criterion for making a theoretical development has been the opportunistic one: A theoretical investigation has been carried out if existing theoretical models have been insufficient to reach the objectives.

1.3 COMPUTATIONAL EXPERIMENTS AND DATA SETS USED

To verify the theoretical hypotheses concerning the decomposition of learning, a series of computational experiments with two classification problems have been performed. Both data sets have been selected to satisfy the following requirements:

1. They have to correspond to real-world problems. This requirement is necessary to ensure that the theory is not verified on a problem that is either positively biased for this theory, or of no practical interest.
2. The ratio of training set size to pattern dimensionality must be sufficiently high to ensure generalization even in the nonlinear case. Otherwise, the classifier tends toward memorizing training patterns without building a generalized representations of whole classes.
3. The data set must be large enough to allow for splitting to a training set and a test set, both of sufficient size. There are techniques for utilizing virtually the entire data set as a training set while still being able to make a full-scale independent verification (e.g., the "leaving-one-out" technique), but they increase the computational costs of the verification immensely.
4. Comparable results from investigations of other researchers for neural and other classifiers should be available. Otherwise, there is a danger that the results reached in this book are far from optimal, which would make all conclusions involved useless.

1.3.1 Thyroid Data

The first of the data sets used for evaluation throughout this book is the thyroid data set. It is a set of clinical diagnostic data and has been given to me by courtesy of Sholom Weiss of Brandeis University. It consists of patient records concerning thyroid disorders in the years 1985 and 1986. A comprehensive series of computational experiments comparing the performance of various classical, symbolic, and neural classification algorithms has been developed by Weiss and Kapouleas [165]. In these experiments the 1985 data have been used

TABLE 1.1 Standard Backpropagation after 2000 Iterations: Misclassification Rates (Percent)[a]

Hidden Units	Training Set	Test Set
2	1.85	3.10
3	1.60	2.95
6	1.15	3.20
9	1.00	3.15

[a]After Weiss and Kapouleas [165].

TABLE 1.2 Standard Backpropagation: Best Misclassification Rates (Percent)[a]

Hidden Units	Training Set	Test Set	Iterations
3	0.50	1.46	70,000
6	0.37	1.63	45,000
9	0.40	1.93	24,000

[a]After Weiss and Kapouleas [165].

as training data and the 1986 data as test data. For comparability reasons, this partitioning has been preserved.

The training set consists of 3772 cases, the test set of 3428 cases. Each case is described by a vector of 21 input values (15 Boolean and six real values) and a correct classification, which is one of three classes: normal, hyperthyroid, and hypothyroid. There is a substantial bias in favor of the normal class—3488 training cases (i.e., 92.47%) and 3178 test cases (i.e., 92.71%) comprise this class.

Of particular importance is the fact that classical linear classifiers have reached misclassification rates as high as 6.25%. Taking into account that only 7.5% of the data are assigned to classes other than normal, we can say that this problem is very nonlinear. The results for standard backpropagation with various numbers of hidden units are presented in Tables 1.1 and 1.2.

1.3.2 Handwritten Digits

Another data set used for evaluation of individual modularization concepts is a large collection of handwritten digits. Both the training set and the test set consist of 1000 examples of each digit. Each digit is represented by $16 \times 16 = 256$ gray values, each ranging from 0 to 255. A series of computational experiments with neural network classifiers and classical polynomial classifiers (see Schürmann [142]) have been run by Kreßel, Franke, and Schürmann [95] and Kreßel [94]. The lowest misclassification rate reached by a multilayer perceptron has been 3.7%, while the polynomial classifier with carefully selected 1075 linear and quadratic features attained an excellent value of 2.3%. This outstanding result, reached at the well-known AEG research laboratory, which has had almost two decades of experience with handwritten-digit recognition, represents a very difficult benchmark. This data set is comparable to the widespread set of 9298 handwritten digits extracted from zip codes collected at the Buffalo post office. This data set has been classified by a multilayer perceptron of sophisticated layer structure at the AT&T research laboratory (LeCun et al. [99]). The best misclassification rates attained have been about 5%. In contrast to the thyroid data, linear classifiers exhibit acceptable performance for this data set. However, it can still be improved substantially by nonlinear classifiers.

For investigations of generalization capabilities of individual modular algorithms, a random choice of 100 samples per digit has been used as a reduced training set. As a test set, all 10,000 test patterns have always been taken. The best results of Kreßel et al. [94] for this reduced set have been 8.9% misclassifications for the multilayer perceptron with 40 hidden units, but over 60% for the polynomial classifiers with 1075 features.

1.4 OVERVIEW OF DECOMPOSITION METHODS

In the preceding section, various aspects of modularization have been presented. Each of the viewpoints—the engineering viewpoint, the complexity viewpoint, and the psychological viewpoint—suggests one or more approaches to the decomposition of learning.

The approach suggested by the neurobiological point of view is that of *decomposition by learning type*. Our everyday observations of human behavior and development as well as of the structure of the human neural system suggest the hypothesis that human learning is not based on a single type of learning, but rather, on a mixture of supervised learning (e.g., learning by instruction), reinforcement learning (learning by good and bad experiences), and unsupervised learning (learning by observation). It could also be observed that while practical learning tasks are usually specified as supervised learning tasks, it is frequently possible to use unsupervised learning to find a data representation that is more advantageous for consequent supervised learning than the original, unprocessed representation. Virtually all known self-organizing principles, such as Kohonen maps or competitive learning, are candidates for such preprocessing.

If we want to select and apply some of these self-organizing principles, we must first formulate more precisely what data representation can be considered as being more advantageous than the original input. There are (at least) two obvious cases:

- A *compressed* representation, which describes the input by substantially fewer features than the dimensionality of the input, but with little information loss
- A *simplified* representation, which enables the use of simpler algorithms for the same tasks

The former approach (pursued in Chapter 5) to finding an advantageous representation of input, the data compression approach, can also be characterized as a feature-discovery approach. It consists of the search for a set of features whose number is substantially lower than the dimensionality of the original data. An important requirement is that the information content of these features not be substantially lower than that of the original data. This is a phenomenon typical of human information processing. We are frequently able to describe in a couple of sentences a visual scene consisting of thousands of pixels so that almost all relevant information is preserved. To be able to do this, a complex system of concepts must be available to us. These concepts are usually developed by observation, in an unsupervised learning mode. It can even be expected that such data compression to features or concepts will contribute to better generalization—the cognitive data processing is "forced" to a view predefined by existing concepts. (For more precise arguments, see Section 3.5.)

A typical instance of the latter approach is that of making nonlinear problems linear. This is, of course, not universally possible, but there are, for example, ways to extend the class of linearly separable problems by appropriate preprocessing. This preprocessing can be performed by unsupervised learning. There are unsupervised learning principles that have the capability of finding regions in the input space in which the inputs are concentrated, and grouping these inputs into clusters of similar patterns. Representing input by membership in these clusters makes the learning more linear than with the original representation. It will be shown in Chapter 6 that preprocessing by these principles can transform even strongly nonlinear problems such as thyroid data classification into linear ones. This, in turn, makes possible the use of more efficient and better generalizing linear algorithms with well-understood convergence properties.

A more formal view, motivated by the complexity aspects of modularization, is the basis of the group of methods attempting the *decomposition of the function to be mapped*. The layered structure of most network models suggests the possibility of decomposing the mapping represented by the network to mappings represented by individual layers and learning these partial mappings separately. This can be done, for example, in the following ways:

1. Boolean functions can be canonized by transforming them into conjunctive or disjunctive normal form (e.g., distribution-free learning, Boolean category learning).

2. In difficult classification tasks, the class regions may be non-convex. Each nonconvex class region can be expressed as a union of convex class regions. Convex regions can be looked for separately (e.g., some of the approaches based on radial basis functions or RCE networks).

3. Higher-order networks represent an attempt to preempt the order of the mapping to be represented by the order of the network. An analogous principle is the basis of classical nonlinear regression and discriminant analysis.

4. The idea of finding salient features of the data that can reduce the dimensionality and simultaneously be helpful in solving a classification or mapping problem can, consequently, be extended to finding statistical features useful for the concrete learning task.

5. Another approach does not decompose the mapping itself but tries to decompose the network to parts that show the fewest mutual interactions during learning.

While the first four approaches represent a kind of conceptual extrapolation of hierarchical feature discovery, the last is an instance of modularization in the sense of system theory. Since the first three approaches have already been elaborated and described extensively in the literature, in this book we focus on the last two.

The last approach is motivated by the engineering style of work. It concentrates on decomposition of the application development procedure rather than decomposition of the network structure. It consists of separating the task of *learning network structure* from *learning network parameters*. This possibility is suggested by the fact that a complete neural network specification consists of two components: a network structure (connectivity) and network parameters (typically, weights and thresholds).

There are several possible strategies for determining network structure:

1. *Prewired Connectivity*. The simplest and currently the most utilized approach is to take a fixed connectivity. While for classification and mapping tasks the connectivity is determined primarily by experience, there are tasks such as vision for which specific structures are inferred from biological knowledge.

2. *Optimizing the Structure*. There are several attempts to optimize the structure explicitly, for example by genetic algorithms.

3. *Task-Specific Structures*. Application tasks can generally be decomposed into subtasks. Individual subtasks can then be assigned to individual subnetworks.

4. *Knowledge-Based Structure Design*. A large domain of neural network applications overlaps with the domain of knowledge-based applications. It is obvious that the quality of neural network applications can be improved if the available knowledge (that would otherwise be encoded in an alternative knowledge-based system) could be drawn upon. While nearly optimal network parameters can be expected to be found through use of a learning procedure, the network structure (which is typically not optimized by learning) could be inferred from the application domain structure. To do this in a well-founded manner, it is necessary to find some interpretation of the network structure in terms of application domain concepts such as causal or local relationships. This interpretation can then be used to pre-

specify the structure (and possibly some of the parameters) of the neural network.

1.5 STRUCTURE OF THIS BOOK

The first part of this book is introductory. In Chapter 2 a brief overview of neural networks is given, with a bias toward principles and models that are useful from the modularization viewpoint. Chapter 3 is concerned with brain structure, function, and information processing.

The second part of the book consists of chapters dedicated to individual approaches to the modularization of learning. In Chapter 4 we introduce the decomposition of learning to parts using different learning types: typically, a supervised learning part and an unsupervised (self-organizing) learning part. Two instances of this approach are presented in Chapter 5 (supporting supervised learning by feature discovery) and Chapter 6 (supporting supervised learning by quantization). The possibilities of discovering features optimal for a given task are discussed in Chapter 7.

Another approach to modularization considers a decomposition of the mapping to be represented by a neural network (Chapter 8). The most obvious application of this idea is decomposition into a linear and a nonlinear mapping component. The topic of Chapter 9 is decomposition of the network that is optimal with regard to interactions between individual subnetworks during learning.

A group of modularization approaches that are oriented to the structure of the application task rather than to the structure of learning are presented in Chapter 10. Finally, decomposition into a knowledge-based part and a learning part is discussed in Chapter 11.

PART I

Neural Networks

CHAPTER 2 ⎯⎯⎯⎯⎯⎯⎯⎯⎯⎯

Introduction to Neural Networks

This book is not intended to provide an overview of neural networks. It concentrates on a particular topic: modular learning in neural networks. On the other hand, it is always useful, in addition, to provide a broader context, which is the goal of the present chapter. It is a (certainly incomplete) survey of some important dimensions according to which neural networks can be classified, rather than an attempt for an overview of current research or even particular models. For an overview of theoretical aspects of neural networks, the reader is referred, for example, to the excellent book of Hertz, Krogh, and Palmer [63].

2.1 SOURCES OF MOTIVATION FOR NEURAL NETWORKS

As in most research fields, the motivation for neural network research consists of many facets. Some of them are biological in nature —explaining how the human brain operates. Others come from artificial intelligence, whose ambition is to understand the principles of intelligent behavior and use them for construction of artificial intelligent systems.

The biological motivation persisted for decades in a rather stable form, being the basis of an equally persistent research effort by such researchers as Grossberg and his group. In contrast, neural network research motivated by artificial intelligence has experienced two tidal waves. The first came at the very beginning of artificial intelligence research in the 1950s. It had its origins in the straightforward thesis that intelligent systems simply *must* be implementable as networks of simple interconnected processing units, as is the case for human and animal brains. The subsequent decline of interest in neural networks is frequently attributed to a well-known book by Minsky and Papert [110]. However, theoretical analyses of that book alone certainly were not sufficient reason for abandoning an entire research field. They were amplified by the frustration of researchers when their high expectations regarding neural network–based artificial intelligent systems had been disappointed.

In the next period, attention focused on a completely different approach. Just as psychology and the cognitive sciences abstract from biological implementation details of mental processes, it was postulated that the microstructure of the computing machinery on which an artificial intelligent system is implemented is to a large degree irrelevant to its behavior. What was supposed to be important was the high level of reasoning. Since reasoning is always connected with symbols, workers concentrated on searching for symbol-manipulating algorithms to use in solving particular tasks, such as recognition, logical inference, or planning.

In this period, symbolic, mostly logic-based models of intelligence reached a high degree of sophistication. They have come to serve as the foundation of an application technology, the technology of expert systems. Special logic systems have also been developed to capture particular features of human reasoning: for example, default logic, temporal logic, and reasoning about beliefs.

If we examine the distribution of capabilities of logic-based reasoning systems and compare them with the human approach to reasoning, we quickly recognize striking differences. Logic-based reasoning exhibits excellent performance in making consistent inferences from sets of logical statements that are huge in size compared with the analogous sets with which humans are able to cope. On the other hand, they may fail to solve even the simplest tasks of everyday life: recognizing faces from various views, bipedal walking on an irregular terrain, planning under uncertain or changing circumstances.

These observations led to a revival of interest in neural networks in the late 1970s and early 1980s. A new hope has arisen that neural networks, more sophisticated than those of the first wave of interest, will be able to alleviate some of the difficulties inherent in artificial intelligence.

This hope originated in several inherent properties of neural network models, of which (1) generalization, (2) graceful degradation, (3) adaptivity and learning, and (4) parallelism are particularly important. In each of the following subsections we discuss briefly one of these properties and its importance for artificial intelligence tasks.

2.1.1 Generalization

An indisputable property of logic-based methods is their rigidness. Logical inferences are performed on syntactically completely defined strings of symbols. Since there is no concept of similarity between the symbols, an arbitrarily small change in input leads to completely different inferences. This property makes it difficult to cope with real-world data and situations. Since no two real-world situations are exactly the same, they must either be described by two different sets of logical expressions, which would lead to completely different inferences for each situation, or abstractions have to be introduced, which would result in equal logical descriptions for similar situations. But then the problem is replaced by the only somewhat simpler problem of choosing an appropriate system of abstractions.

It is obvious that for real-world data, some type of continuous representation and inference system is required, with similarity metrics such that for similar inputs or situations, outputs or inferences are similar, too. This is an inherent property of neural networks with continuous activation units. Even networks of discrete units can exhibit continuous behavior in statistical terms if they are composed of large numbers of units. These properties let us expect a smooth generalization from stored cases to new ones.

2.1.2 Graceful Degradation

The problems noted associated with generalization become even worse if data are inaccurate or incomplete. Although inaccurate data are always in the near neighborhood of exact data, a logical inference system, because it lacks a similarity concept, may lead to results that differ to a disastrous extent from those corresponding to exact data. This is typical of the behavior of logic- or rule-based expert systems. Their knowledge bases contain syntactically encoded knowledge about cases that have been considered as typical at the moment of expert system design. If some of the inputs are inaccurate or missing, the expert system's reaction may be completely nonsensical because the inference chain cannot be used in the same way as with exact data.

This is not the case for neural networks. If a small proportion of the input data is missing or distorted, performance deteriorates only slightly. Performance deterioration is proportional to the extent of data inaccuracy or incompleteness.

2.1.3 Adaptivity and Learning

The theory of logic is concerned with the task of drawing sound inferences from a given set of logical statements rather than with the question of how this set is generated. Although there are also some interesting theoretical results in inductive learning, the question of practical knowledge acquisition, that is, acquisition of general statements from individual cases in a real-world context, is an unsolved problem.

Similar difficulties arise with expert system maintenance. If the environment changes slightly, there are no feasible methods of incremental adaptation to such a modified environment. This is an important handicap since few tasks are invariant in time.

By contrast, for most neural network models, learning by presentation of individual cases is the *only* way of encoding knowledge into them. Adaptation is very straightforward, too. In fact, there is no strict difference between learning as an initial knowledge acquisition on the one hand, and adaptation as a process of maintenance of acquired knowledge in changing conditions on the other.

2.1.4 Parallelism

Logical inference procedures are mostly sequential. A set of valid logical statements is scanned for syntactical patterns that would allow the application of an inference rule. By this inference rule, a new valid logical statement is deduced and inserted into the set. This step is iteratively repeated until a given goal is satisfied (e.g., a given query answered). Convergence to the ultimate goal can be ensured only by keeping the process in a consistent line of argument, for example, by consistent variable instantiations. Otherwise, the inferences would produce an exploding quantity of true but useless statements. If multiple inferences are to be performed simultaneously, they have to be checked carefully for possible interferences.

The computational expensiveness of automatic reasoning systems induced a considerable research effort in the field of parallelism. Several parallel reasoning models have been developed and implemented (e.g., Concurrent Prolog, Parlog). Examining these sophisticated systems, we realize how difficult the task really is. Although it is frequently possible to search simultaneously through disjunctive branches of the search tree ("or-parallelism"), parallel inferences on conjunctive branches ("and-parallelism") have generally to be supported by the user, for example, by saying which variables have to be bound and which not. For such specifications, considerable skill is necessary.

This contrasts with the inherent parallelism of virtually all neural network algorithms. In most cases, all units, or at least large groups of them (e.g., layers) can be updated simultaneously, or even in an asynchronous mode. This property of neural networks is important from the implementation viewpoint. Since it is increasingly difficult to speed up single processing units, the only alternative solution is to distribute computationally expensive tasks to large numbers of such units working in parallel.

2.2 BASIC COMPONENTS OF NEURAL NETWORK MODELS

Let us now discuss briefly the principal constituent parts of a neural network model. For more complete and more general treatment, the reader is referred to introductory books on neural networks, for example that of Rumelhart and McClelland [140, Chap. 2].

For a neural network model to be specified completely, we have to define its *physical parts*, and the necessary *algorithms*. Like any other network or graph, a neural network consists physically of *nodes*, or *processing units*, and *edges*, defining its *topology*, or connectivity.

Any information-processing system has to be provided with a processing algorithm. Neural networks allow only for algorithms that can be performed by (mostly very simple) communication between (equally simple) processing units. In most cases the entire abstract algorithm can be reduced to a *propagation rule*. Complete specification of the information-processing algorithm requires definitions of all three components mentioned: the functionality of processing units, topology, and propagation rule. Another algorithm required for any information-processing system concerns some type of *programming* of the system, that is, specifying the information-processing algorithm that is to be applied. In neural networks, this task is solved by learning, mostly summarized into a relatively simple *learning rule*.

2.2.1 Processing Units

Processing units of a neural network are artificial counterparts of neurons in a brain. Like any other processing devices, they can be viewed as some type of automata. Therefore, information processing in them is described completely in terms of:

- Input into the unit from other processing units or from the environment
- Output sent to other processing units or to the environment
- The unit's internal state
- The rule for computing the next state from the current state and the current input
- The rule for computing the output from the current state

The internal state of a processing unit is usually referred to as the unit's *activation*. Correspondingly, the rule for computing the next state of the unit is called an *activation rule* or activation function. This basic structure of a processing unit is given in Figure 2.1.

Since inputs, outputs, and states of biological neurons are represented by physical magnitudes, their most appropriate modeling is by continuous values. This is also the prevailing approach to artificial neurons. Furthermore, using continuous inputs, states, and outputs supports building smooth similarity metrics in the neural network. Therefore, it is consistent with artificial intelligence–based motivation for neural network research discussed in the preceding section, in particular with the goals of graceful degradation.

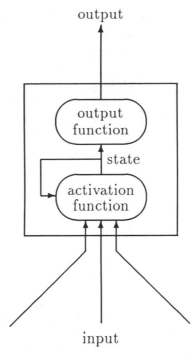

Figure 2.1. *General scheme of processing unit.*

Biological neurons are complicated physical systems. Complete descriptions of their inputs, outputs, and states would be by long vectors of membrane potentials and other physical and chemical magnitudes. A realistic description of the dynamic behavior of each single neuron would certainly consist of a large number of nonlinear partial differential equations. Even if our state of knowledge permitted us to formulate such a complete model, it is very probable that its complexity would make analytical treatment impossible. The consequence would be that we would not be able to figure out even the most elementary features of the neuronal dynamics from this description. So there is strong motivation for simplification of the neuronal model. A widespread means of simplification is to describe each of the basic functional modes—(1) the processing mode and (2) the learning mode—by a separate model.

The *processing state* is typically reduced to a single activation value. This state can be viewed as a *short-term memory*. Its dynamics are described by a single differential equation. The output is in many cases simply set equal to the state. Some widespread models, such as the perceptrons, went even one step further. Their processing units do not have any genuine state—their output is a simple function of their current input. This function is based primarily on the simplified neuron model of McCulloch and Pitts [107]. Its simplest version is a step function,

$$f(x,\sigma) = \begin{cases} 1 & \text{if} \quad x > \sigma \\ 0 & \text{otherwise,} \end{cases} \tag{2.1}$$

of the weighted sum of individual inputs. To make the activation function differentiable, the step function was later replaced by the so-called sigmoid function,

$$f(x,\sigma) = \frac{1}{1 + e^{-(x-\sigma)}}. \tag{2.2}$$

(The differentiability of the activation function is crucial for the application of gradient learning methods such as the widespread back-propagation method.) In some cases, even a linear function is sufficient to replace the step function. Combining inputs into a weighted sum has become so usual that it is frequently taken for grant, and the term "activation function" is used in the restricted sense, denoting the function through which this sum is passed, such as the step or sigmoid function. The scheme of such a simplified processing unit is shown in Figure 2.2.

As we can see, the processing state is equivalent to the state of activation of a simplified artificial neuron. By contrast, the *learning state* is characterized by a vector of parameters of the activation function. These parameters change gradually during the lifetime of the neural network, optimizing its performance with regard to some performance criterion. This is why the learning state can be viewed as a formal counterpart of *long-term memory*. For the simplest versions of neuronal models mentioned above, the parameters of an activation function consist of:

1. Weights of individual inputs, with the help of which the weighted sum is computed
2. A threshold of the step or sigmoid function

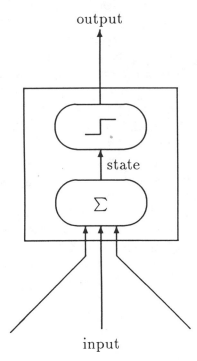

Figure 2.2. *Simplified processing unit.* Additive input + threshold *function.*

Note 2.2.1   Since each input to a processing unit of a neural network corresponds to a connection to another processing unit, the
weights can alternatively be assigned to the connections themselves
instead of being viewed as parameters of the activation function.
This arrangement is consistent with the widespread interpretation
of weights as *connection strengths*. An argument in favor of the view
used here is that both processing and learning are implemented within the processing units. The processing units are then the only active
elements of a neural network, the function of network connections
being reduced to defining the topology.

2.2.2 Topology

In the preceding subsection, a widespread type of processing unit
with a single-valued activation state has been presented. It is obvious that the computational power of each such processing unit taken
alone is rather limited. It is considerably lower than that of even the

simplest modern pocket calculator. If a system made of such processing units has to solve complex tasks in a way reminiscent of human cognitive capabilities, its sophistication must consist of something different from that of the processing units themselves—namely, their interactions.

It is the topology of a neural network that determines which interactions can take place and is thus of crucial importance for the performance of the network.

Although the connections can be defined as either directed or indirected, the directed case is more convenient. It defines immediately the inputs into a processing node. It also allows for an asymmetric case in which connections are not identical in both directions. Symmetry can always be materialized by thinking of each indirected connection as a pair of directed connections.

The simplest case is certainly a *completely interconnected network* (see Figure 2.3). This case is also the most general, since the nonexistence of a particular connection can always be emulated by omitting this connection from the activation function of the processing unit the connection enters, or by setting the corresponding weight to zero. This topology also allows for arbitrarily complex feedback structures.

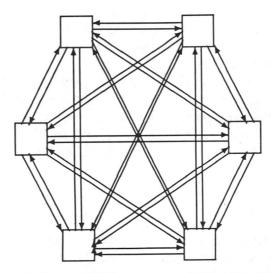

Figure 2.3. *Completely interconnected network. Bidirectionality of connections is symbolized by pairs of edges.*

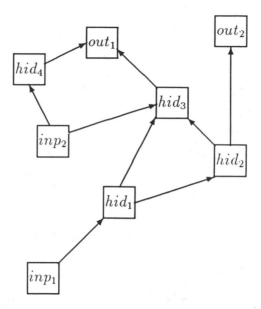

Figure 2.4. *A feedforward network.* $inp_{1,2}$, *input nodes,* $hid_{1,2,3,4}$, *hidden nodes;* $out_{1,2}$, *output nodes.*

Although feedback extends the class of possible behaviors enormously, it may also be harmful in some cases. In particular, feedback may lead to slow convergence, even lack of guaranteed convergence in the processing mode. (In the learning mode, convergence may be a problem even without feedback.) So in some cases it may be desirable to exclude the possibility of feedback on the topology level. The way to reach this is simple. The network has to be an acyclic graph; that is, it must be impossible, following any path along directed connections, to enter a unit once left. Such a network, called a *feedforward network*, is shown in Figure 2.4. In completely interconnected networks, all units may have both connections entering and leaving the unit. By contrast, in feedforward networks we can always identify *input units* (i.e., units with no connections entering them) and *output units* (i.e., units with no connections leaving them). It follows from the properties of directed graphs (which a feedforward network is) that each unit can be assigned a rank giving the number of units on the longest path between it and some input unit. The acyclic property implies that the longest path is finite. For obvious reasons, for any pair of interconnected units, the rank of the unit the connection

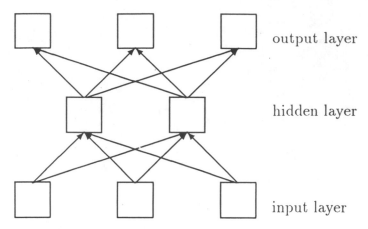

Figure 2.5. *Layered feedforward network.*

leaves is lower than the rank of the unit the connection enters. For simple processing units without an internal state (except for activation function parameters), each unit's activation can be computed after a number of iterations equal to the unit's rank. Consequently, the network can be completely evaluated after a number of iterations equal to the maximum rank of the network.

The scheme for iterative evaluation according to the rank of individual units suggests aggregating units into subsets of equal rank. With the further restriction that the rank difference between interconnected units always be 1, we receive a *feedforward layered network*. An example of this network type is presented in Figure 2.5. It can be evaluated in a number of iterations, equal to the number of interconnection *layers*. The kth layer consists of the connections between the units with ranks k and $k - 1$. The evaluation can be viewed mathematically as a sequence of vector operators. The simplest case, that of a single-layer feedforward network, is the topology used by one of the first neural network models, the perceptron of Rosenblatt [136].

However, not all layered networks are necessarily feedforward. If we allow the connections to be bidirectional, we receive *feedback layered networks*. Examples of such networks are the adaptive resonance theory (ART) of Grossberg [50] and the bidirectional associative memory of Kosko [93].

2.2.3 Propagation Rule

Given a description of processing units and topology, the network is ready for information processing. The only thing that remains to be specified is at which time and in which order unit activations are updated. The approach that is probably closest to the natural biological system is simultaneous and *asynchronous* update of all units. This approach would allow real-time processing of a continuous input stream without a supervision device.

However, in addition to the possibility that brain activity is less asynchronous than it may appear at first glance, it is difficult to emulate an asynchronous device on our carefully synchronized computers. Since there are also no obvious functional advantages of the asynchronous approach, most existing propagation rules are *synchronous*.

Another important network model feature with consequences for the propagation rule is whether the network is feedforward or feedback. For feedforward networks, the basic steps in the processing algorithm are the following:

1. The input pattern is represented by input units by setting their activations to the values of corresponding pattern elements.
2. In the kth step, the activations of units of rank k are computed. (It makes no sense to compute them earlier since the activations of some of their predecessor units may not yet have been determined.)
3. After the number of steps equal to the highest rank in the network, the state of output units corresponds to the output pattern.

For feedforward layered networks, the algorithm is modified as follows:

1. The input units are set equal to the input pattern.
2. In the kth step, the activations of units of the kth layer are computed using the activations of the $(k-1)$th layer.
3. After a number of steps equal to the number of layers, the state of the output units corresponds to the output pattern.

The processing can be viewed as a spread of activation from layer to layer. Obviously, the evaluation of a feedforward network can be viewed as the evaluation of a nested nonrecursive function.

The situation is completely different for feedback networks. The functionality of input and output units is not as distinct as for feedforward networks. In most nonlayered feedback networks such as the Hopfield network (Hopfield [69]) or the Boltzmann machine (Ackley et al. [3]), any unit can become input or output. Although propagation rules for feedback networks are more varying than those for feedforward networks, many of them are instances of the following *relaxation* framework:

1. The input pattern is *clamped* to the corresponding units; that is, the activations of these units are fixed to the values corresponding to the pattern elements.
2. All units, except for the clamped units, are iteratively updated.
3. Iterative updating is stopped after the activations of all units have reached some kind of stationary state or after a predefined number of iterations.
4. The output pattern is read from the corresponding units.

The stopping rule depends greatly on the network model. For some models or configurations, convergence or even stability may not be guaranteed.

2.2.4 Learning Rule

The most difficult constituent part of a neural network model is the learning rule. Since it also operates on a network of interconnected units, it formally resembles the propagation rule: It consists of changing the state of individual units (the state of activation function parameters, in this case) using inputs from the neighboring units. The particular form of this rule is very variable, and even an enumeration of its basic classes had to be omitted for space reasons.

Only one feature common to many models will be mentioned here. Most learning rules are modifications of stochastic gradient optimization of a certain objective function or performance criterion. Although this is well known regarding the error backpropagation algorithm of Rumelhart, Hinton, and Williams [139], it is also (sometimes nonintentionally) the case for such models as the following:

- The perceptron of Rosenblatt [136], minimizing a differentiable modification of the Bayesian misclassification rate.
- The Boltzmann machine learning algorithm of Ackley, Hinton, and Sejnowski [3], minimizing the difference between probabilities of unit activations in clamped network states and probabilities in nonclamped states.
- The unsupervised learning rule of Oja [114], minimizing the difference between the original pattern and the pattern reconstructed from its feature representation.
- The self-organizing rule for quantization of Kohonen type [92], minimizing the distance of patterns from the cluster centroid.

Another aspect of learning rules, their classification according to learning type, is the topic of a future section.

2.3 KNOWLEDGE REPRESENTATION

From the viewpoint of artificial intelligence, the question of knowledge representation is of crucial importance. In traditional artificial intelligence (AI), knowledge representation is based on symbols. Symbols provide many natural ways of representing knowledge explicitly: by rules, logical expressions, or even natural language sentences.

Originally, supporters of the neural network approach claimed that it could solve AI problems on the subsymbolic level of sensory signals and patterns of activity. However, if higher-level cognitive tasks such as language understanding and production were to be addressed, the neural network community split into two parts, differing in their opinion of how far tasks of a symbolic nature can be reduced to subsymbolic ones. These two opinions lead to two proposals for knowledge representation principles:

- Local representation.
- Distributed representation.

2.3.1 Local Representation

The local approach to knowledge representation is a straightforward extension of traditional AI models. It assigns one processing unit to each symbolic concept. From the representational viewpoint, there is a strong relationship to graph-oriented AI approaches such as semantic or Bayesian networks. Even the inference mechanisms are sometimes very close to each other, both being based on relaxation-type algorithms. (This topic is treated in depth in Chapter 11.)

A clear advantage of this approach is its direct correspondence to the concepts of the task to be solved. Another advantage is the transparency of the network. If each unit is assigned a concept, a connection between two units can be assigned a relationship between both corresponding concepts. The causal or probabilistic strength of this relationship can be expressed by the connection strength. So both topology and network parameters can be determined and interpreted.

On the other hand, there is a price to be paid for this convenience. The assignment of concepts to processing units must be done manually. It is difficult to find general principles for creating new concepts if it turns out to be necessary during learning. Consequently, learning is limited to optimizing network parameters, such as connection weights or thresholds. This fact narrows the scope of possible generalization from examples. What does not fit the framework of predefined concepts and corresponding processing units cannot be properly represented and generalized. To summarize: Local representation is appropriate if a substantial amount of explicit knowledge is available.

2.3.2 Distributed Representation

In contrast to one-to-one mapping between processing units and concepts in local representations, distributed representation is characterized by concepts corresponding to patterns of simultaneous activity of several units.

Although such networks are less transparent than localist ones, their flexibility in *creating* representations for new concepts is much greater. Whereas for local representations it must be decided explicitly when to create new concepts (see Hinton et al. [66]) and when to assign a new processing unit, concepts as activity patterns may emerge gradually in distributed representations. Such emergent concepts can frequently be found by simple learning algorithms such as the gradient method.

Another property of distributed representations, the *coarse coding* property [66], is of importance for graceful degradation. If pattern sets for which individual processing units are activated overlap, the resulting representation is simultaneously very smooth and highly accurate, although the accuracy of each processing unit is limited. The accuracy arises through the collaboration of many units and can be explained in the following way. Let us view the inaccuracy of each unit as a random variable. The variance of this random variable is a measure of the expected average inaccuracy of this unit. The measure of inaccuracy (i.e., variance) of a pattern consisting of a weighted sum of activations of many processing units is, relative to its magnitude, substantially lower (by the square root of their number) than the inaccuracy of individual units.

2.4 LEARNING TYPES

Different formulations of learning from examples provide different amounts and forms of information about the individual examples and the goal of learning. There are three large classes of such formulations of learning:

- Supervised learning.
- Unsupervised learning.
- Reinforcement learning.

Although this classification applies to learning generally, rather than being specific for neural networks, it will be mentioned here because of its importance to the principal topic of this book, the modularization of neural network learning.

2.4.1 Supervised Learning

One extreme on the scale of the quantity of information supplied is supervised learning. It is characterized by knowing exactly what response has to be associated with each pattern. For classification, it is the exact class of each pattern. For functional mapping, it is the function value. For forecasting, it is the forecast value.

If the association is completely predefined, it is easy to define an error metrics (e.g., mean-squared error) of the associated response. This in turn gives us the possibility of comparing the performance with the predefined responses (the "supervision"), changing the learning system (a neural network in our case) in the direction in which the error diminishes.

2.4.2 Unsupervised Learning

Another extreme in the quantity of information supplied is no information. This type of learning is called unsupervised learning. Since the system is given no information about the goal of learning, all that is learned is a consequence of the learning rule selected, together with the individual training data. This is why this type of learning is frequently referred to as *self-organization*.

What, if anything, can be learned by such a learning system? Primarily some type of *regularity of data*, such as membership in clusters of similar patterns or highly correlated features. The associations found by unsupervised learning define representations optimized for their information content. Since one of the problems of intelligent information processing deals with selecting and compressing information, the role of unsupervised learning principles seems to be crucial for the efficiency of such intelligent systems.

2.4.3 Reinforcement Learning

The third type of learning is a combination of the other two. In reinforcement learning, each pattern is provided with information (in a supervised manner), but this information is very restricted in form. It consists merely of a statement as to whether the response associated with a particular pattern (as it has been generated by the learning system in a certain stage of learning) is "good" or "bad." The learning algorithm has to make the best of this information, typically by simply making good associations more probable. It is frequently conjectured that this is the type of learning that is the most proximate to the learning in living organisms.

A number of reinforcement learning algorithms has been developed in the field of learning automata (see Narendra and Thathachar [112]), some of which have been adapted for neural networks. Many of these algorithms have well-understood convergence properties. On the other hand, it is to be expected that the restricted information has a negative impact on both quality of solutions and convergence speed. So it is always advisable to prefer supervised learning algorithms if complete information is available.

2.5 SOME IMPORTANT MODELS

Let us now review some of the most important existing models. The goal of this chapter is to illustrate some of the aspects of neural network taxonomy presented in previous chapters. Neither the selection of models nor their order should suggest any assessment of their importance. Many sophisticated and influential models have been omitted because of their complexity or simply for space reasons.

2.5.1 Perceptron and Adaline

One of the first (and still important) models ever proposed is the perceptron of Rosenblatt [136]. Its primary goal has been the classification of visual patterns. A similar approach has been pursued by Widrow [168] (see also Widrow and Smith [169]). The perceptron is a single-layer feedforward network with a layer of input units and a single output unit. All inputs are weighted by a vector of connection strengths and fed into a step function. So the activation function of the output unit is

$$z = \delta \left(\sum_i w_i x_i - \sigma \right)$$

$$\delta(x) = \begin{cases} 1 & \text{for} \quad x > 0 \\ 0 & \text{otherwise} \end{cases}$$

(2.3)

with x_i being the ith element of input patterns, z the output, w_i the connection weight of the ith input, and σ the output unit's threshold. The output unit activation can obviously assume only two values, zero and 1. Each value corresponds to one of two pattern classes that have to be separated.

The learning rule of the perceptron is supervised. It consists of a very simple and intuitively clear strategy of changing the weights only if the pattern **x** is misclassified, that is, if the activation of the output unit for this input pattern is not equal to the correct class of the pattern. The amount of change is

$$\Delta w_i = \begin{cases} x_i & \text{if} \quad \text{class} = 1 \\ -x_i & \text{if} \quad \text{class} = 0. \end{cases} \tag{2.4}$$

This simple learning rule has an important property. If both classes are linearly separable, the weights will converge to the values materializing this separation.

While the perceptron rule solves the problem of separating linearly separable pattern classes, it does not reach a stable state for linearly nonseparable classes. The *Widrow–Hoff rule* [170], also called the *delta rule*, has different properties. Instead of a step function in the activation function of Rosenblatt's perceptron, it uses simply the identity function (i.e., the activation of output units is equal to the weighted sum of inputs):

$$z = \sum_i w_i x_i - \sigma. \tag{2.5}$$

This rule consists of changing the weights in the direction of the steepest gradient of the error function:

$$E = (z - d)^2 \tag{2.6}$$

with d the correct class (0 or 1). The rule can be written

$$\Delta w_i = (d - z)x_i. \tag{2.7}$$

Since the error function (2.6) is convex, the gradient method converges to the global minimum. So the rule minimizes the quadratic error between the correct and forecast class in the 0–1 representation and thus is equivalent to the formulas of linear discriminant analysis. On the other hand, it does not guarantee the separation of linearly separable classes.

2.5.2 Multilayer Perceptron

The single-layer perceptrons described above suffer from a serious limitation. They can only build linear separating hyperplanes, and thus can separate only linearly separable classes. This limitation, pointed out by Minsky and Papert [110] at the end of the 1960s, led to a substantial decrease in interest in neural network research.

A way to overcome this limitation was proposed by Werbos [166] and formulated in the *backpropagation learning rule* of Rumelhart, Hinton, and Williams [139]. The backpropagation model is based on two principles:

- To overcome the limitations of the single-layer perceptron, all that is necessary is to insert one or more additional layers between input and output. These layers consist of processing units with nonlinear activation functions, typically sigmoid functions (2.2). Arbitrary convex classes can be separated by a network with one such hidden layer (a two-layer network), and arbitrary nonconvex classes by a network with two hidden layers (a three-layer network); see, for example, Lippmann [102].
- The delta rule (2.7) can be used to learn output layer weights. Remaining weights can be learned by recursive application of the chain rule for computing derivatives. For a two-layer network with x_i representing input unit activations, y_j hidden-unit activations, z_k output unit activations, w_{kj} output layer weights, and v_{ji} hidden-layer weights, the rule is the following:

$$\frac{\partial E}{\partial v_{ji}} = \sum_k \sum_j \frac{\partial E}{\partial z_k} \frac{\partial z_k}{\partial y_j} \frac{\partial y_j}{\partial \sum_i v_{ji} x_i} \frac{\partial \sum_i v_{ji} x_i}{\partial v_{ji}}$$

$$= \sum_k \sum_j (z_k - d_k) w_{kj} y_j (1 - y_j) x_i \qquad (2.8)$$

Recursive formulas are given in [139].

These simple principles have constituted a very successful model that is the basis of a large number of applications.

2.5.3 Madaline

Another approach to extending the computational power of the perceptron has been proposed by Widrow. To attain the capability of nonlinear separation, multiple Adalines (perceptron-type units) are arranged in a layer and classification is done by a "majority vote." The learning rule for the multiple Adaline (Madaline) is based on the idea that each Adaline unit should become responsible for a certain region in the pattern space. In a certain stage of the learning process, there are units with firm votes (i.e., far from the threshold) and others with undecided votes (in the neighborhood of the threshold). In the case of a misclassification, only the least decided Adaline unit's weights are changed.

2.5.4 Radial Basis Networks

Step and sigmoid functions for processing unit activation can be imagined to be a kind of logical detector. If most class features, corresponding to the strengths of connections entering the unit, are sufficiently strong for a unit's threshold to be exceeded, the pattern class defined as a conjunction of these features is recognized. There is also an alternative view. A class of patterns can be seen as a template, or point in the pattern space. A pattern class is assigned to this class if it is sufficiently near this template. The usual metric of proximity is Euclidean distance.

These arguments suggest using another type of activation unit, the *radial basis unit*. This unit is activated if the input pattern is in the neighborhood of a point assigned to this unit. The simplest form of such an activation function has been used in the RCU network of Reilly, Cooper, and Elbaum [130]:

$$
f(\mathbf{x}) = \begin{cases} 1 & \text{if } \sum_i (x_i - s_i)^2 < r \\ 0 & \text{else.} \end{cases}
\tag{2.9}
$$

This function is a certain analogy of the step function (2.1). It is equal to 1 if the pattern is in the hypersphere of radius r around the template $\mathbf{s}$, and to zero otherwise. The coordinates of the template play the role of connection weights for step functions. More flexible than a circular region is a oval region. It can be implemented by introducing weights t_i into (2.9):

$$f(\mathbf{x}) = \begin{cases} 1 & \text{if } \sum_i t_i(x_i - s_i)^2 < r \\ 0 & \text{else.} \end{cases} \tag{2.10}$$

To make this function continuous and differentiable, a Gaussian-type function can be used instead of (2.9):

$$f(\mathbf{x}) = e^{-\sum_i (x_i - s_i)^2}. \tag{2.11}$$

The relationship between this function and the function (2.9) is analogous to the relationship between the sigmoid function (2.2) and the step function (2.1).

2.5.5 Adaptive Resonance Theory of Grossberg

Conventional computers store data in the same way as we store things in a cellar. The data are put in their entirety at certain physical sites in memory and can always be found there unless they are explicitly erased. This simplistic procedure cannot be applied if we expect the memory (1) to generalize and (2) to find representations more efficient than storing each pattern entirely, as is expected from neural network memories.

Both requirements can be formulated as a mathematical objective function and a more or less satisfactory solution found. For example, if the task is classification, it is sufficient to store the information relevant for assigning each pattern from the training set to the corresponding class.

This task becomes much more difficult if the system has to operate incrementally. The main problem is that there is no explicit training set that would define the distribution of data on which the system is to perform optimally. A trivial but hardly practicable solution would be to store all patterns ever met and to recompute the representation periodically. Otherwise, one faces a formidable problem of how new patterns are to be assimilated into the existing framework without the risk of modifying this framework so substantially that past information is lost.

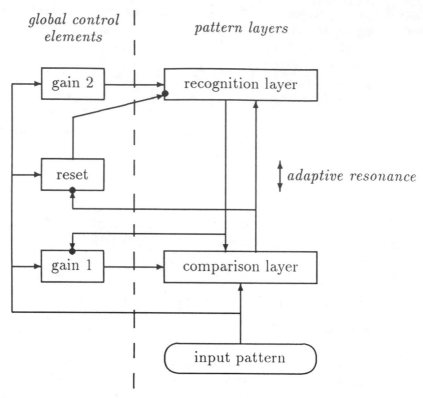

Figure 2.6. *Adaptive resonance theory network. Inhibitory connections are indicated by filled circles.*

This problem, known as the *stability–plasticity dilemma*, has been addressed by Grossberg [50]. The solution is a model called *adaptive resonance theory (ART)*, developed further by Carpenter and Grossberg [24]. It is a network with the structure shown in Figure 2.6. It is a layered, feedback network for unsupervised learning. It has two layers: (1) the comparison layer and (2) the recognition layer. Additionally, there are three control elements: (1) gain 1, recalling the input pattern in the comparison layer; (2) gain 2, "priming" the recognition layer on arrival of an input pattern, and (3) reset, coming into action if a new pattern is dissimilar to all previous ones.

Operation of the network can be described roughly as follows:

1. An input pattern is fed into the comparison layer and then sent to the recognition layer.
2. The new pattern is compared with the patterns stored in the recognition layer and the recognition layer pattern with the highest similarity is chosen as a candidate for the category of the new pattern.
3. If the candidate category pattern is sufficiently similar to the new pattern, the candidate category is modified in the direction of the new pattern (assimilation), and the new pattern is viewed as an instance of this category.
4. If the similarity is below a certain threshold defined by the vigilance parameter, the new pattern becomes a new category of its own.

This scheme solves the stability–plasticity problem. Whereas patterns that can be assigned to some of the known categories improve the definition of these categories incrementally, completely unknown patterns, which could be expected to disturb the previous knowledge seriously if forced to assimilate, constitute new categories.

2.5.6 Kohonen's Feature Maps

One step of the adaptive resonance theory algorithm consists of the selection of the category unit that shows maximum response to a given pattern. Only this maximum response unit is then really activated. This can be viewed as competition between the category units for activation. This competitive principle is a basis of an entire class of neural network models, a prominent example of which is Grossberg's adaptive resonance theory. Another prominent example is the model of Kohonen, known as self-organizing feature maps [91]. Feature maps are single-layer, unsupervised learning networks. Although their original, biologically oriented form included lateral feedback in the output layer, the basic functionality can also be reached by a reduced, feedforward model.

The original motivation for this model has been biological. It has been shown that some brain regions are ordered in a particular fashion: Signals that are physically similar, such as similar frequencies of acoustic signals or even similar geographical locations in the organism's environment, activate neurons proximate to each other. In other words, neurons of these regions are ordered to reflect the topology of the signal space (see [91, p. 120]). Feature maps represent an attempt to explain this phenomenon.

Feature maps differ from previous examples by a particular arrangement of the output or feature layer. The output layer is not viewed as a simple set of processing units but as a neighborhood system. The neighborhood system defines the functional similarity between individual processing units of the feature layer. Units that are close in this neighborhood system are expected to react to similar input patterns.

This behavior is induced by a special learning algorithm, which can be summarized in the form of three rules. As in the ART model, each feature unit is characterized by a template pattern.

1. For each feature unit, the similarity of its pattern $\mathbf{p}_j$ to the input pattern $\mathbf{x}$ is computed:

$$y_j = \|\mathbf{x} - \mathbf{p}_j\|. \tag{2.12}$$

   The unit with the highest similarity is activated.

2. The parameters of the activated unit are changed by the rule

$$\Delta \mathbf{p}_j = \alpha \mathbf{x} - \mathbf{p}_j. \tag{2.13}$$

3. The parameters of the *neighbors* of the activated units are changed by the same rule, with a lower value of the learning rate α.

The first two rules implement competitive learning. The last rule, which enforces correlated activities of neighbor units, is responsible for the *topological self-organization* of the layer. Particularly interesting are mappings between spaces of different dimensionalities: for example, the mapping of a three-dimensional physical space to a two-dimensional representation.

2.5.7 Adaptive Rule of Oja

An important unsupervised learning principle has been discovered by Oja [114]. It is a modification of the famous Hebbian learning rule [61]. One of the forms of the Hebbian rule is the following:

$$\Delta w_{ji} = \alpha y_j x_i \qquad (2.14)$$

with y_j and x_i unit activations and w_{ji} the connection weight. It is obvious that this rule lets the connection weight converge to the statistical correlation between activations of both units.

Oja's modification is the following:

$$\Delta w_i = \alpha(y x_i - y^2 w_i). \qquad (2.15)$$

In contrast to the original Hebbian rule, this learning rule is asymmetric with regard to the units x_i and y. These units are assigned different roles. Unit x_i is one of a set of input units, representing an element of a certain input vector. There is a single output, or feature, unit y. This unit is activated by a linear activation rule

$$y = \sum_i x_i w_i. \qquad (2.16)$$

The topology of the corresponding network is equal to that of a single-layer perceptron—it is a single-layer feedforward network.

Without further information about the input pattern (i.e., in an unsupervised manner), learning rule (2.15) is applied. An interesting property of this learning rule is the convergence of the weight vector to the first principal component of the input. This means that the feature unit y corresponds to the statistically most significant linear combination of input pattern elements. The m-dimensional input space is compressed into a one-dimensional space.

2.5.8 Hopfield Network

All networks treated so far have been instances of layered networks. By contrast, the networks presented in this and the following subsections are nonlayered networks. The Hopfield network [69] is a set of completely interconnected processing units with a perceptron-like activation function

$$z_j = \delta \left(\sum_{i \neq j} w_{ji} z_i + x_j - t_j \right) \qquad (2.17)$$

with

$$\delta(x) = \begin{cases} 1 & \text{if} \quad x \geq 0 \\ 0 & \text{else,} \end{cases}$$

x_i being an external input into the ith unit.

If the activations of all units are iteratively recomputed using this activation function, the network state will relax to a certain stable state, depending on the external inputs x_i and, of course, on the weights w_{ji}. This state can be characterized as a minimum of a certain function, frequently called an *energy* or *Liapunov function*.

The Hopfield network has an interesting property. Let us have a set of patterns that we want to be "stored" in the Hopfield networks. The ith element of the hth pattern will be denoted as y_{ih}. If the weights are determined as

$$w_{ji} = \sum_h y_{jh} y_{ih} \qquad (2.18)$$

(i.e., as a correlation of corresponding pattern elements), the relaxation procedure of Section 2.2.3 will, under certain conditions, converge to the pattern that is most similar to the pattern given as the external input. In particular, if the external input is an *incomplete* pattern from the stored set, the network will converge to its *completed* form. This justifies the Hopfield network as a model of associative memory.

2.5.9 Boltzmann Machine

The deterministic character of the Hopfield network has a harmful consequence. The state to which the network converges corresponds merely to a *local* minimum of the energy function. If we take into account that for associative memory, there is generally no guarantee that the local minimum is also a global minimum, this property is a severe limitation of the applicability of the model. This limitation is overcome by a similar but probabilistic neural network model, the Boltzmann machine (see Ackley et al. [3]). The activation function of the Boltzmann machine is described by the *probability of activation* of the jth processing unit,

$$P_j = \frac{1}{1 + e^{-(\sum_{i \neq j} w_{ji} z_i - \sigma_j)/T}}, \qquad (2.19)$$

with T a constant, frequently referred to as "temperature." Note the similarity to the sigmoid activation function of multilayer perceptrons (2.2). Processing units for which there are external inputs are "clamped"—committed to these external values.

The most important feature of the Boltzmann machine network model is the *annealing algorithm*. Instead of performing relaxation with a constant activation function, the activation function is modified by letting the temperature parameter T gradually decrease from an initially high value to zero. The sense of this procedure becomes clear if we investigate the probability (2.19) of high and low temperatures. For a high temperature, the term in the exponent is near zero and the entire probability approaches $\frac{1}{2}$, whatever the activations z_i of remaining units may be. In this state the network performs a random search with a low bias toward low-energy states but with a wide scope of search. The probability of being trapped in a local minimum is low. By contrast, if the temperature approaches zero, the probability of activation is heavily dependent on the value of the sum in the exponent. If this sum exceeds the unit's threshold σ_j, the probability approaches unity. If the sum is below the threshold, the probability is near zero. This behavior can be viewed as a commitment to a local minimum and fine tuning of the solution.

2.6 TASK TYPES THAT CAN BE SOLVED BY NEURAL NETWORKS

The goal of neural network application research is to find models that can solve useful tasks. The variety of neural network models as well as the variety of terminology used may make identification of such tasks difficult. The objective of this section is to present the most important classes of *application tasks* that neural networks are able to solve. A related but different question of *theory overlapping* with other research fields is addressed briefly in the next section.

2.6.1 Functional Approximation

Every deterministic feedforward network represents a certain mapping of the input, materialized by the layer of input units, to the output, materialized by output units. This mapping can be evaluated by propagating the activations from the input layer toward the output layer.

The class of functions that can be represented by a network is determined by the network topology and activation functions. For example, the output of a single-layer perceptron with a linear output unit results from the input vector **x** in the following way:

$$y = \sum_i w_i x_i. \tag{2.20}$$

Obviously, a linear perceptron is capable of representing the class of all linear mappings.

It is much less clear which class of mappings can be represented in the multilayer perceptron. However, practical experience has shown that even a two-layer perceptron with relatively few sigmoid hidden units, formally written as

$$y = \sum_k w_k sig \left(\sum_i v_{ki} x_i \right), \tag{2.21}$$

is astonishingly successful in approximating a broad, although still formally unidentified class of functions, or functionals. In addition to single-layer and multilayer perceptrons, layered feedforward networks with radial basis activation functions seem to perform particularly well for general functional approximation tasks.

Functional approximation is a general theoretical framework for several application-oriented tasks. Probably the most important of these are:

- Classification.
- Control.

Theoretically, any network model (as well as any other mathematical model) for general functional approximation is applicable to classification and control. However, specific properties of these two applications require particular activation functions and learning rules.

2.6.1.1 Classification.

Most currently existing applications of neural networks can be characterized as classification tasks. The term "classification" is not always used for the same task type. In this paragraph we are considering supervised classification, in contrast to unsupervised classification (characteristic of, for example, Grossberg's models). Even the scope of the term "supervised classification" must be somewhat restricted. For example, classification of *structured objects* still goes beyond the state of the art of the current neural network models. So the classification task will be characterized in the following way:

- Let us have a set of *objects*, each characterized by a fixed-length vector of numeric or Boolean *features*, and a set of *classes* such that each object is assigned to exactly one class.
- Let us further have a subset of this object set, called a *training set*, for which the class assignment is explicitly known.
- The neural network can be *trained* to estimate the class of objects that have not been members of the training set.
- The performance of a neural classifier is measured by the proportion of objects for which their class assignment estimate has been correct (*the recognition rate*).

The feature vector describing the objects is frequently referred to as a *pattern* and the entire task as *pattern recognition*. An important subclass of classification tasks are medical or industrial *diagnostic tasks*. Objects represent diagnostic cases, features correspond to symptoms or measurements, and classes are assigned to particular diagnoses. Most feedforward network models, including the perceptrons, Adaline, Madaline, and others, have been developed explicitly for classification as a goal application.

2.6.1.2 Control.

Another important instance of the general mapping task is the control task. For a given device, called a *plant*, to be controlled, a *controller* is to be designed that affects the behavior of the plant in some desirable way, for example, by stabilizing it or keeping it on a certain trajectory. To do this the controller is provided with information about the state of the plant. Formally, the controller design amounts to seeking a mapping

$$\mathbf{u} = f(\mathbf{z}) \tag{2.22}$$

with $\mathbf{z}$ the vector of plant state variables and $\mathbf{u}$ the vector of controller actions. This mapping has to be optimal with regard to some objective function, or at least satisfy certain requirements.

So far, the task is completely within the framework of a typical functional approximation task. However, the problem is in supplying information about the success of control so that this information can be exploited by a supervised learning algorithm. The straightforward approach of observing a model controller and sampling input–output pairs (pursued, for example, by Widrow and Smith [169]) is scarcely of practical value since typically, no model controller is available.

So the focus of research in neural network models for control is on looking for new frameworks in which efficient learning can take place. Examples of these approaches are the adaptive critic approach of Barto, Sutton and Anderson [12], backpropagation critic of Werbos [167], dual backpropagation of Munro [111], and backpropagation in time of Nguyen and Widrow [113].

2.6.2 Data Compression

Functional approximation, with its instances of classification and control, are typical supervised learning tasks. By contrast, data compression is an application of unsupervised learning. For a given set of data patterns, compact representation is sought. In such a compact representation, each pattern is compressed to a pattern whose dimension is substantially lower than that of the original pattern. The task of a neural network model applied to data compression is to find a mapping that reduces the original pattern to a compressed pattern.

The learning rule of Oja [114] given in Section 2.5.7 is a neural network model for linear data compression. For nonlinear data compression, multilayer perceptrons in an autoassociative mode can be used: The desired output of the perceptron is set equal to the input. If an autoassociative perceptron with a hidden layer that is narrower than the input (and output) layer is trained to produce outputs that are very close to the inputs, the hidden layer constitutes a nonlinear compression of input patterns. The inverse mapping of compressed patterns to the original ones is given by the output layer. Data compression models are discussed thoroughly in Chapter 5.

2.6.3 Clustering and Quantization

The clustering task can be formulated in the following way: A given set of objects, characterized by a fixed-length vector of features, is to be partitioned into a certain number of subsets, or *clusters*, such that the variability of objects within each cluster is low, while the variability between the clusters is high. This task can also be viewed as an extreme form of data compression. The information about the object is compressed into the identifier of the cluster to which this object counts. The cluster identifier may be, for example, a natural number. Despite such an extreme degree of compression, this information may be very significant if combined with a description of the cluster (e.g., by the coordinates of its centroid).

The fact that continuous pattern features are transformed to a discretized or "quantized" description by cluster characteristics justifies the alternative denotation of this task: *quantization*. Clustering tasks can be solved using competitive learning rules such as those of Grossberg (Section 2.5.5) or Kohonen (Section 2.5.6). Quantization is treated in detail in Chapter 6.

2.6.4 Topological Mapping

Besides their clustering capabilities, Kohonen's feature maps of Section 2.5.6 are able to solve another interesting task. They can find a mapping of a (continuous) input space to the (quantized) output space such that topological properties such as the neighborhood in the input space are preserved in the output space. As mentioned in Section 2.5.6, of particular interest are mappings between spaces of different dimensions.

2.6.5 Optimization

In Section 2.2.3 a general propagation procedure for feedback networks called *relaxation* has been described. This procedure can be viewed as a minimization of a certain global function of activations of all processing units of the network. This suggests the possibility of solving a minimization (or generally optimization) problem by relaxing an appropriate feedback network. This has really been the case for some applications such as the traveling salesman problem solved by Hopfield and Tank [70]. With probabilistic neural networks and a special version of relaxation, the *annealing procedure* (see Section 2.5.9), even a statistical convergence to global optima can be guaranteed.

On the other hand, not all optimization problems are suitable for the neural network approach. The class of optimization tasks that can be solved by relaxation of annealing can be characterized by the following properties:

- A *neighborhood* system must be defined on the variables of the optimization task.
- The objective function to be maximized has to be *additive* in terms of *cliques*, groups of variables within which each variable is a neighbor of every other variable.

A rigorous formulation of these properties is by means of a random Markov field and the theory of Gibbs sampling (Geman and Geman [45]).

The simplest case of cliques is that of variable pairs. The optimization function must then be additive in terms that depend on only two variables. For the Boltzmann machine, these terms are products of activations of two units multiplied by the weight of the connection between the two units.

As in the case of functional approximation, optimization is a very general task. It has a number of subclasses, which can themselves be viewed as task classes. Those tackled most frequently by neural network approaches are (1) maximum-likelihood data interpretation, and (2) associative memory. An overview of neural networks optimization methods and their applications is given, for example, by Hertz, Krogh, and Palmer [63, Chap. 4].

2.6.5.1 Data Interpretation. For this special case of an optimization task, the objective function is a joint probability function over a certain system of random variables. Suppose that some variables are known to have certain observed or measured values. Maximizing the joint probability can then be viewed as looking for the global state of all variables that is maximally consistent with the observed values. This is desirable in many optimal decision problems, such as diagnostic tasks. A neural network model for this task is presented in Chapter 11.

2.6.5.2 Associative Memory.

An associative memory is a memory from which stored data are retrieved by specifying a part (or a distorted form) of these data rather than an explicit key under which the data are stored. This task can obviously also be formulated as a pattern completion task. If the retrieval key is a part of the data or their distortion, it has to be specified how large this part has to be, or to what extent the distortion can differ from the original data. In both cases some kind of distortion measure must be defined. This distortion measure is mostly defined locally (i.e., by the distance of corresponding elementary data items or "microfeatures"), and it is usual to define the overall distortion measure as a sum of such distances. With such a distortion measure, the retrieval consists of finding the data for which the distortion is minimal. The additiveness requirement is obviously satisfied. So the associative memory retrieval is an instance of a class of optimization tasks solvable by neural network approaches.

Associative memory as a model of human memory has always been a favorite topic for neural network researchers. Some neural network models have been designed explicitly with this goal in mind. The most prominent of them are the Hopfield network [69], the Boltzmann machine [3], and bidirectional associative memory [93].

2.7 RELATIONSHIP TO OTHER RESEARCH FIELDS

The goal of neural network research is to study how various types of intelligent behavior can be implemented in systems made of neuronlike processing elements and brainlike structures. Many aspects of intelligent behavior have also been studied in other disciplines. It is thus natural to expect that researchers in those fields arrived at results similar to those of neural network researchers. In this section a short and certainly incomplete review of some related fields of research is presented. It is my opinion that establishing such relationships is very useful for both neural networks and related disciplines. It can prevent neural network research from "reinventing the wheel" and help focus on topics that are really innovative. Simultaneously, it can provide new insights into traditional disciplines.

2.7.1 Discriminant Analysis

Statistical discriminant analysis is concerned with the problem of optimal classification under certain assumptions about the statistical distribution of patterns within classes. It is one of the most prominent groups of methods for pattern recognition and is even frequently used as a synonym for pattern recognition.

The simplest and most widespread is *linear discriminant analysis*. Its most important result is that if the distribution of patterns within each class is *Gaussian*, with *equal autocorrelation matrices* for all classes, the optimal Bayesian classifier (i.e., the classifier with the minimum expected misclassification loss) is

$$W = C_{yx}C_{xx}^{-1} \tag{2.23}$$

with x representing input patterns; y, vector coding of the pattern's class (with unity in the class position and zeros in the remaining positions); C_{yx}, the matrix of correlations between y and x; and C_{xx}, the autocorrelation matrix of x. This formula is formally equivalent to the formula for minimum-squared-error linear approximation of a mapping:

$$y = f(x).$$

As stated in Section 2.5.1, the delta rule (2.7) represents gradient descent for the quadratic error function (2.6). Since this error function is convex, the gradient method is guaranteed to find the minimum. But this minimum is exactly equal to the weight matrix computed by formula (2.23). Consequently, classifiers trained by the delta rule are equivalent to those of linear discriminant analysis.

If the assumption of equal variance for all classes is relaxed, the optimal Bayesian classifier is quadratic. This is the motivation for quadratic, or generally polynomial, discriminant analysis (see, e.g.,

Schürmann [142]). An analogous argument has been pursued by Pao [118] through his functional-link nets. The advantage of the discriminant analysis approach is the availability of the exact analytical formula (2.23), instead of an iterative and thus less exact, and probably also slower, neural network with delta rule training. On the other hand, we have to keep in mind the restrictions under which this result is valid—Gaussian distributions with equal autocorrelation matrices for all classes. This assumption does not seem likely to hold in many practical cases. If these assumptions are violated, the linear discriminant classifier is not optimal. Even worse, it does not guarantee separating the classes if they are linearly separable. In this case neural networks with error functions *different from the delta rule* [e.g., the perceptron rule (2.4)] may be superior to the discriminant analysis. This topic is treated in depth in Chapter 6.

2.7.2 Cluster Analysis

The goal of cluster analysis has been characterized in Section 2.6.3 as partitioning a given set of patterns into a certain number of clusters such that the intracluster variability is low while the intercluster variability is high. The intracluster variability can be measured by

$$E = \sum_h \sum_k \sum_i (x_{hki} - \overline{x}_{hi}) \tag{2.24}$$

with h the cluster index, k the index of patterns within a cluster, i the index of the pattern vector element, and $\overline{x}_{hi}$ the mean value of the ith element of pattern vectors in the hth cluster. The measure of intercluster variability is

$$B = \sum_h \sum_i (\overline{x}_{hi} - \overline{x}_i) \tag{2.25}$$

with $\overline{x}_i$ the mean value of the ith element of pattern vectors over all clusters. The sum of E and B is equal to the total variance:

$$T = \sum_h \sum_k \sum_i (x_{hki} - \overline{x}_i) \tag{2.26}$$

and is thus constant for all decompositions of the data set. So the clustering task can be formulated as a minimization of intracluster variance E over all possible partitionings of the data set into the clusters.

There is no general method for finding the global minimum, but some simple and fast methods for finding a local minimum have been proposed. The best known of these is the *k-means method* (see, e.g., [7] or [55]). It consists of iteratively performing two steps:

1. Computing centroids of currently defined clusters
2. Reassigning patterns to the clusters so that each pattern is in the cluster whose centroid it is nearest to.

The relationship of the k-means method to competitive algorithms of the Kohonen feature map type (see Section 2.5.6) has been pointed out by Lippmann [102]. The second step of the k-means method is obviously equivalent to competitive selection of the maximum activation processing unit. The only difference in the first step is that while the k-means method computes the centroid of each cluster *explicitly*, competitive learning rules *incrementally change* the parameter vector of the processing unit *toward the centroid*. This is why equivalent results can be expected from both the classical and neural approaches.

As stated by Lippmann [102], Grossberg's form of the competitive algorithm (see Section 2.5.5) has its counterpart in a classical clustering algorithm, the *leader algorithm*.

2.7.3 Principal Components Analysis

In many situations we have to do with objects or patterns described by very large numbers of features. It is then always an attractive possibility to search for other, not directly measurable features, whose number would be substantially lower but which would in some way preserve most of the information contained in the original pattern. This task is obviously closely related to the data compression task of Section 2.6.2.

If we consider all such secondary features that can be expressed as linear combinations of input features, and adopt the variance of input features as a linear measure of information, the task can be formulated as finding $n < m$ (m being the dimension of input patterns) linear combinations of original features that would explain a maximum of variance of the original features. A solution to this task is provided by principal components analysis. The n linear combinations with the maximum information content are equal to the n eigenvectors of the input autocorrelation matrix with the largest absolute values of the corresponding eigenvalues.

For the self-organizing rule of Oja [114], convergence to the first principal component has been proven. Generalizations of this rule are discussed in Chapter 5.

Since most of the methods used for computation of eigenvectors are iterative rather than based on explicit formulas, the rule of Oja and its generalizations can be viewed as useful alternatives to such methods.

2.7.4 Regularization Theory

A typical formulation of a functional approximation task is to minimize the mean error of the functional values for a given set of input–output pairs. This formulation is satisfactory if either the task is really confined to the given input–output pairs, without any ambition to generalize to novel patterns, or the number of input–output pairs is sufficient to represent the mapping very densely. Otherwise, the approximation may become ill defined—it will not work in gaps between the patterns by which it has been constructed. To overcome this ill-definedness, further assumptions about the mapping have to be made. This is the concern of regularization (or spline) theory. The usual expression, based on quadratic error, is extended by a regularization term,

$$E = \sum_i (z_i - d_i)^2 + \lambda \|Pz\|^2, \qquad (2.27)$$

with P being a differential operator, d_i the desired output, and z_i its approximation. In the simplest case of P being a second derivative, the regularization term forces changes in the derivative to be small in absolute value.

Poggio and Girosi [128] pointed out the relationship between a class of regularization algorithms and neural networks based on the radial basis function (2.10). The simplest case consists of assigning a processing unit to each pattern and taking the pattern coordinates as a center of the corresponding radial basis function. For this case, an explicit solution for output layer weights is

$$\mathbf{w} = (\mathbf{H} + \lambda\mathbf{I})^{-1}\mathbf{d} \tag{2.28}$$

with $\mathbf{d}$ the vector of desired outputs and $\mathbf{H}$ the matrix of values of all radial basis functions for all patterns.

A more general case of number of radial basis functions less than the number of patterns can be solved by a generalized radial basis function with moving centers adaptively determined by a gradient method [128].

2.7.5 Automata Theory

Learning automata are theoretical models for devices that improve their performance in their environment. A learning automaton is characterized by the following features:

- *Input* from the environment
- *State*
- *Output* to the environment

State and output can be assigned values from predefined finite sets. This is also the case for input in so-called P- or Q-automata, while input of S-automata is allowed to be continuous between 0 and 1.

The input from the environment is typically restricted to information about the desirability or quality of the current state of the environment. The output of a learning automaton represents an action of the device on the environment. The goal of learning is to iteratively identify the action that is most favorable with regard to inputs from the environment.

In the theory of learning automata (see, e.g., Narendra and Thathachar [112]) many learning rules and analyzed, some of which have mathematically proven convergence. This theory also provides interesting insights into the nature of learning. One of the most astonishing ones might be the fact that under certain conditions it is more advantageous to reward good actions and to do nothing for bad actions than to reward good and punish bad actions.

The input–state–output scheme and the simple structure of learning automata suggests a strong relationship to processing units of neural networks. The learning by information restricted to one-dimensional evaluation of the automaton's performance is a clear counterpart of reinforcement learning in neural networks. The main difference from neural network reinforcement schemes (e.g., Barto et al. [12]) is that evaluation of action quality is *the only* input of an automaton from the environment. Consequently, the task is limited to selecting the best *universal action* rather than to finding the best *strategy* of reacting to varying inputs from the environments. However, the latter task is treated by a part of learning automata theory under the concept of environment *context*. Less general models are concerned with nonstationary (e.g., periodic) environments with a finite number of possible states.

Particularly interesting seems to be the idea of interconnected automata and their relationship to game theory (Narendra and Thathachar, [112, Sect. 8]). This is a topic barely touched upon in current neural network theory.

2.7.6 Computational Vision

Computational vision has to cope with a number of mathematical problems. Some of them are ill-posed; that is, the information delivered by the sensory input is not sufficient to determine a unique interpretation of the input. Examples of such problems are edge reconstruction and evaluation of optical flow (Wechsler [164]). It is frequently possible to add some supplementary constraints that should be violated as little as possible, such as requiring edges to be straight or the movements suggested by optical flow to be consistent in some neighborhood. Such weak constraints can be summarized in a single objective function.

Geman and Geman [45] have developed the theory of Gibbs sampling, which provides an annealing algorithm for finding a global minimum of such objective functions. The conditions under which this algorithm can be applied have been summarized in Section 2.6.5. These conditions are in most cases easily satisfied for objective functions formulating computation vision problems. The reason for this is the natural definition of neighborhood in visual images.

This algorithm is closely related to the annealing algorithms of feedback neural networks such as Boltzmann machines. Although designed for computational vision problems such as edge completion, this algorithm has become an important part of neural network theory. Convergence of both research fields is to be expected in the future. With deepening of our knowledge of the structure of natural visual systems, the computational vision algorithms are likely to profit.

CHAPTER 3 ——————————

Structure of the Brain

One of the goals of neural network research is understanding how biological neural systems operate. Also, for an engineering-oriented researcher, knowledge of processes within biological systems provides the most important suggestions for proposing artificial neural network models. In this chapter we address in a very brief and simplified fashion some aspects of the structure and function of vertebrate neural systems. Emphasis has been laid on modularity and structural aspects.

The brain is modular on at least three levels:

1. The macrostructure level of brain organization
2. The microstructure level of organization of each brain region
3. The level of structure of individual neurons

We address only the first two levels. The overall structure of brain is the topic of Section 3.1. Brain is presented as a system of interacting modules, or brain regions. Each region has its own microstructure of various cell types and their connectivity. Some examples are given in Section 3.2.

Outstanding brain researchers such as John Eccles and Gordon Shepherd have formulated some general principles of brain organization. Some of them are presented in simplified form in Section

3.3. Even more valuable for an engineering-oriented neural network researcher are neuronal circuits that perform well-defined functions; Section 3.4 presents some examples. An important global aspect of brain data processing is the information-theoretical aspect, which is the topic of Section 3.5.

3.1 MACROSTRUCTURE OF THE BRAIN

The human brain is a system with a complex anatomical, histological, and functional structure. The three principal parts of the brain are (Rexrodt [131]):

- The *brain stem*, divided into the *medulla*, *pons*, *midbrain*, and *cerebellum*.
- The *thalamus* and *hypothalamus*.
- The *cerebrum*, consisting of the left and right *hemispheres* connected by the *corpus callosum*. The largest part of the cerebrum consists of the *cortex*. An important functional cerebral complex is the *limbic circuit*, in particular the *hippocampus*.

Although we are still far from having clarified the function of the brain as a whole, hypotheses supported by experimental evidence concerning the role of individual brain regions can be formulated. In the following sections, supposed functions of some important regions are presented.

3.1.1 Cerebellum

The cerebellum is responsible for precise coordination of movement. While rough commands for voluntary movements seem to have their origin in the motor cortex, the role of the cerebellum is to control the coordinated and precise execution of these commands. Further functions of the cerebellum are (Shepherd [147]):

- Maintenance of posture and balance
- Maintenance of muscle tone

The cerebellum is connected to many other brain regions. For example, it receives inputs from the cortex and basal ganglia (rough motor commands) and the spinal cord (sensory information) and sends outputs to the thalamus and the motor neurons via reticular formation (precise motor commands) (Rexrodt [131]).

3.1.2 Thalamus

The thalamus plays a central role in the processing of sensory inputs. Except for olfactory inputs, all sensory signals pass through the thalamus to be further relayed to individual regions of the cortex. There are also connections in an inverse direction from cortical areas to the thalamus. The sense of this bidirectional connection with cortical sensory areas is assumed [131] to be in *focusing* on sensory inputs that are currently of interest to the individual. This seems to be related to the information filtering function of the brain addressed in Section 3.5. Another function in which the thalamus is assumed to participate is *emotional evaluation* of sensory inputs as positive or negative. This evaluation is crucial for the survival chances of the organism.

3.1.3 Hypothalamus

The hypothalamus is a brain center for *vegetative* and *hormonal* functions. It participates in various processes, such as sleep, growth, sexual behavior, tonus, and so on. Rexrodt [131] formulated the central role of the hypothalamus in regulation of internal processes in the human body in the following way.

1. Internal sensory information (e.g., from intramuscular sensors) ascends via the spinal chord and brain stem to the hypothalamus.
2. Reaction patterns and situational evaluations are retrieved from the memory of these patterns, localized in the hippocampus.
3. Problem solving is done by the cortex, with which the hypothalamus communicates via the thalamus.
4. Commands concerning hormonal actions are communicated to the hypophyse.

Processing of external sensory information may follow a similar pattern except that the sensory input path leads directly to the thalamus instead of being relayed by the hypothalamus.

3.1.4 Cortex

The cortex is the physically largest part of the brain. It consists of about 9 million neurons (Rexrodt [131]). Its various areas are responsible for many activities, among which are:

- Sensory processing of all modalities
- Associative memory of sensory patterns
- Voluntary motor commands
- Memory of motor patterns
- Speech generation
- Planning and logical inferences

In other words, the cortex participates in practically all aspects of intelligent behavior. It also maintains specialized communication pathways with all other brain regions. While the functionality of some parts of the cortex (e.g., retina) has been described in a detailed manner, other aspects, such as temporal planning and logical inferences, remain obscure.

3.1.5 Hippocampus

The hippocampus is classified as a part of the cortex called the *archicortex*. Its seems to play a crucial role in certain types of memory operations. Rolls [135] formulated the following hypotheses about the role of the hippocampus in cooperation among brain regions:

- The hippocampus is responsible for, or even the site of, *episodic memory*, the memory for entire events, including their spatial and temporal context. This hypothesis is suggested by hippocampal damage studies. For example, a consequence of such damage can be the inability to recall associations between objects and their locations. There is also anatomical support for this hypothesis. Hippocampus inputs cover a broad scope of cortical areas and can thus represent conjunctions of various aspects of an episode.
- Another function of the hippocampus seems to be the optimization of storage in cortical memory areas. Its property of having

access to all the information enables it to identify useful conjunctions over the entire information space.

A corresponding neuronal circuit is proposed in Section 3.4.3.

3.2 MICROSTRUCTURE OF BRAIN REGIONS

The anatomical macrostructure of the brain in its use as a system of processing modules is not the only structural level in the neural system. There are at least two additional levels: the structure of a single neuron and the structure of a brain region.

A very simplified structural description of a single neuron is the following. A neuron consists of three parts, each of which can be assigned an elementary information-processing role:

- There are branching fibers called *dendrites*, collecting the *input* into the neuron.
- The cell *body* is responsible for a certain *data-processing* operation. This operation corresponds to the activation function of artificial neural networks (see Section 2.2.1). A usual assumption is that it can be approximated by summing all inputs and passing them through a threshold function. A more realistic assumption is that the sum of inputs has a nonlinear (e.g., sigmoid) influence on the *firing rate* of the neuron.
- A long branching fiber, the *axon*, relays the activation of the neuron to other neurons. It plays the role of an *output* component.

This view of the neuron is very simplified but sufficient for the objective of this chapter, which focuses on structures made of neurons rather than on the structure of the neuron itself. For more details the interested reader is referred to such books as [29] and [147].

Another level of brain microstructure is that of the individual regions. Each region consists of several neuron types, with different characteristics and connectivity patterns. Input into the region is constituted by incoming fibers from other regions or sensory organs. The processing is done by *intrinsic* neurons, also termed *local* neurons or *interneurons*. The output from the region is the task of *principal* or *projection* neurons that send long axons to other regions. Let us exemplify the richness of this structure by the cerebellum, the motion coordination center of the brain.

3.2.1 Structure of the Cerebellum

The structure of the cerebellum has been studied by Cajal [21], Eccles, Ito, and Szentágothai [30], Shepherd [147] and others. It can be summarized in the following way. Input into the cerebellum is by two types of fibers, *climbing fibers* and *mossy fibers*. These inputs come from the spinal cord, brain stem, and cerebral cortex via such regions as the inferior olivary complex and reticular nuclei. There are several types of intrinsic neurons: *granule cells*, *Golgi cells*, *stellate cells*, and *basket cells*. Projection neurons of cerebellum are *Purkinje cells*.

A simplified connectivity scheme of cerebellum (considering only Purkinje, granule, and basket cells) is given in Figure 3.1. It can be characterized by the following features:

- Climbing fibers directly excite Purkinje cells, while mossy fibers excite granule cells, which in turn excite Purkinje cells.
- Climbing fibers also excite basket cells, which in turn inhibit Purkinje cells.

Although Purkinje cells are excited by both climbing and mossy fibers, there is an enormous difference between the pathways. There are approximately as many climbing fibers as Purkinje cells, and we can say roughly that one climbing fiber excites one Purkinje cell. By contrast, each mossy fiber branches to about 1000 granule cells, and each granule cell has excitatory connections to about 300 Purkinje cells. Consequently, each Purkinje cell receives signals from about 300,000 mossy fibers. This is obviously an enormous potential of weight combinations, capable of representing genuinely any mapping necessary for precise motor control.

This arrangement inspired Albus [4, 5] to propose an artificial neural network called the cerebellar model articulation controller (CMAC). CMAC is a powerful model for functional approximation and has been applied to robotic problems (Miller et al. [109]; Graham and D'Eleuterio [47]).

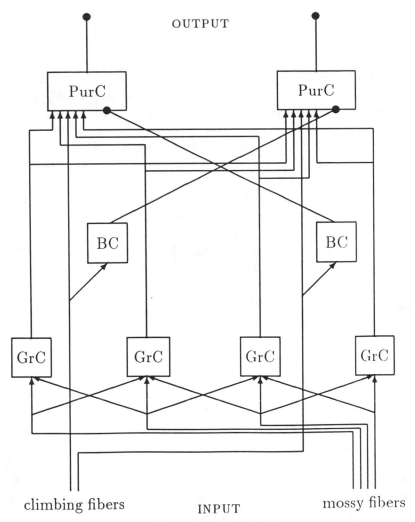

Figure 3.1. *Basic structure of cerebellum circuit. Strongly simplified. Excitatory synapses are symbolized by an arrow, inhibitory ones by a filled circle.*

3.3 FUNCTIONAL PRINCIPLES

Brain research has reached the stage at which individual observations can be summarized into general principles. As in other scientific disciplines, general principles cannot be *deduced*, only *induced* from observations. It is a property of every induction (except for mathematical induction on natural numbers) that its validity cannot

be guaranteed. We can never be sure that examples we have observed have been representative of the entire space of observations.

However, inducing general principles is the only way of compressing the vast quantity of experimental data into something that can
be communicated to other specialists. This is even more true for
communication from neurobiologists to engineering-oriented artificial neural network researchers, who may have problems with a single understanding of the description of neurobiological experiments
and their results.

In this section we give several examples of general principles that
can be helpful in determining a direction for fruitful research on
artificial neural networks. All examples selected are positioned on
the structural level of brain circuits. There are, of course, plenty of
valuable general principles on other levels, including:

- The principle of approximate *additiveness of synaptic inputs* on
  the level of function of single neurons
- The principle of *genetic determinism* of brain structure (Eccles
  [29]), concerning evolution and growth of the brain

3.3.1   Group Activity

The hypothesis of group activity of motor cortex neurons has been
formulated by Eccles [29] and supported, for example, by experiments of Evarts [34]. In the experiments, the activities of two neighboring motor neurons during certain movements have been measured. For a given elementary motion such as flexion or extension of
a certain muscle, sites of activity could be identified. If elementary
motion corresponding to the given site is performed, neighboring
motor neurons exhibit *correlated* firing activity. If measurements are
made on a different site, the activities of motor neurons are not generally lower but are *uncorrelated*. A hypothesis suggested by these
findings is the following: The motor neurons have a strong tendency
to fire spontaneously (firing that cannot be directly assigned to a certain motor action), but if they perform the action for which they are
responsible, they fire in entire neighborhood groups or columns. The
reason for group activity may by the inability of a single neuron to
instigate significant muscle contraction.

What consequence can this finding have for research on artificial neural networks? We begin with the fact that neural network models can be formulated on various levels, in particular:

- On the level of entire neuronal layers, examples of which are the models of von Seelen and Mallot [143] applied to robotic vision
- On the level of groups of neurons (an aspect frequently stressed by Grossberg, for example in [51])
- On the level of abstract neurons such as threshold units (the mainstream of current neural network research and applications)
- On the level of models of realistic neuron behavior (followed recently by many researchers, such as Beer [16])

The question is always which level is relevant for modeling a certain type of behavior. The group activity principle would support the second approach, at least for motor problems. It implication may be that a model of group dynamics of a set of neurons (possibly described in statistical terms) is an appropriate model for motor tasks. It is important to point out that this hypothesis does not in any way preclude the usefulness of the remaining three levels. First, it is not known whether it can be generalized to nonmotor cortical regions. Second, to determine group dynamics of neurons, a lot has to be known about the dynamics of individual neurons. For this goal, the simplifications underlying the definition of "abstract neuron" (see Sections 3.2 and 2.2.1) do not provide for the *variability* of behavior observed in biological neural systems.

3.3.2 Competition

The principle of group activity makes neuronal activity strong and coherent. There is also another principle that is helpful in maintaining coherence, the competition principle. It has been observed (Eccles [29]) that while the activities of neurons of one motor cortex column are reinforced by a positive loop, the activity in neighboring columns is inhibited. A neural mechanism for this is by lateral inhibitory connections from basket cells to the pyramid cells (projection neurons of motor cortex) of neighboring columns.

A similar pattern of connectivity can be observed in the cerebellum (see Section 3.2.1). Input fibers (climbing and mossy fibers) excite both granule cells and basket cells. Basket cells spread their axons, called *parallel fibers*, to adjacent cerebellum regions. Purkinje cells (cerebellar projection neurons) are excited by granule cells but inhibited by parallel fibers from basket cells of adjacent regions.

Both principles, reinforcement of excitation of a column and lateral inhibition, result in permanent *competition* between cell groups or columns. By interaction of both principles, only activities with genuinely strong support from sensory input (or input from other brain regions) can persist. This improves the coherence of neuronal activities and prevents the organism from performing contradictory actions simultaneously.

The competition principle has been addressed by many neural network researchers. Grossberg [50, 51] has shown that the competitive principle can be used for pattern classification and, in combination with a learning rule, for the learning of categories. Kohonen [91] identified a mechanism for forming topology-preserving maps, also using the competitive principle.

3.3.3 Increasing Specificity

Rolls [135] has formulated a hypothesis that the specificity of reaction of neurons to individual sensory patterns grows with the processing stage. Specificity can be measured by the "breadth of tuning index" proposed by Smith and Travers [150]. This index is, in fact, an entropy measure. It takes values between zero, for a completely specific response to a single pattern, and 1, for a completely unspecific response to all patterns.

Evidence in favor of this hypothesis comes from two sensory areas:

- In the taste system the breadth of tuning index decreased from 0.870 initially for the *nucleus of the solitary tract*, to over 0.665 for the *operculum* and 0.563 for the *insula*, to 0.389 for the caudolateral orbitofrontal taste area of the cortex.
- In the visual system, increasing specificity for *pattern classes* such as faces has been observed. Although no cells responding specifically to a single face have been found, there are cells that respond very specifically to certain subsets of faces and hardly respond at all to nonface patterns.

The increasing specificity principle is important for designing artificial neural network systems. It implies that it may be advisable to decompose the process of, for example, visual pattern recognition to stages of increasing specificity. This can be accomplished by incrementally building in more and more specific invariants of individual pattern classes. This approach has also really been pursued by neural network researchers, in particular by Fukushima et al. [41] in his neocognitron and in the industrial application of handwritten zip code recognition by LeCun et al. [99].

3.4 FUNCTIONAL CIRCUITS

General information-processing principles discovered in the brain are an important source of inspiration for artificial neural network research. Another source are individual neuronal circuits, about which neurobiologists acquired such detailed knowledge that they have been able to identify the *functionality* of these circuits. In this section we present three examples of such circuits described by Eccles [29]:

1. The servomechanism of muscle control in the spinal chord
2. Cerebellar loops
3. A circuit described by Rolls [135] involving processing stages in the hippocampus

3.4.1 Muscle Control

The structure of the muscle control circuit is shown in Figure 3.2. The muscular part of the circuit consists of a *muscle spindle* and an *extrafusal muscle*. It is the latter part whose contraction is the goal of a motor action. The spindle contains sensors whose signals are lead by *Ia fibers* to α *motor neurons*. Spindle sensors will fire if the spindle is stretched by external forces or if the spindle contracts, and will stop firing after loosening the spindle: for example, if extrafusal muscle contracts without simultaneous contraction of the spindle. Firing of α motor neurons is transmitted via α fibers to extrafusal muscle and causes its contraction. *Intrafusal fibers* of muscle spindle can be brought to contraction by γ *motor neurons* via γ fibers. Both α and

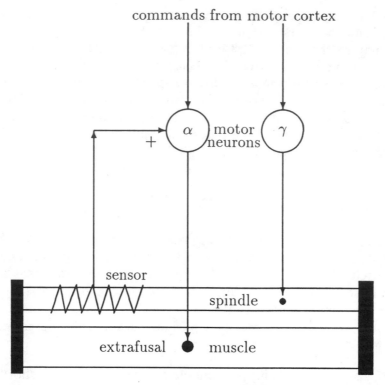

Figure 3.2. *Muscle control. Spindle and extrafusal muscle are simultaneously stretched or contracted. For details, see the text.*

γ neurons receive inputs from the pyramidal cells of motor cortex. These inputs can be viewed as motor commands.

This leads to the following behavior:

- If the muscle is stretched by external forces, for example by a load, the spindle stretches, α neurons are activated by *Ia* fibers, and the muscle contracts automatically to trade-off the stretch. After the trade-off, the spindle is no longer stretched and extrafusal muscle stops contracting.
- If the γ neuron is activated by motor commands from pyramid cells of the motor cortex, tensing occurs in the spindle and the extrafusal muscle contracts by the mechanism described above.
- If γ and α neurons are activated by motor commands simultaneously, the servo γ circuit plays the role of pacemaker for the ef-

fector α circuit. If the contraction of extrafusal muscle is smaller than that of muscle spindle (which can be caused, for example, by an unexpected load), the γ circuit increases the activation of α neuron and thus muscle contraction.

The experiments of Vallbo [158] have shown that this mechanism is actually used for voluntary movements. The α activation is immediately followed by correcting operations of the γ loop.

3.4.2 Cerebellum Loops

The cerebellum is one of the brain regions whose structure and function are best understood. It is natural that in a region such as the cerebellum, consisting of about 30 billion neurons (probably the largest quantity in the entire human brain), knowledge of individual circuits down to the level of individual neurons is not as detailed as in the case of muscle control by spinal cord motor neurons. Nevertheless, this knowledge has been sufficient for John Eccles to propose a rough functional model of two control loops:

- A closed loop including the motor cortex, the *pars intermedia* of the cerebellum, and components for physical interaction with the organism's environment—muscles and sensors
- An open loop consisting of the association cortex, cerebellar hemispheres, and motor cortex

Both loops have been chained into a broader proposal of motion control proposed by Allen and Tsukahara [6].

The simplified scheme of the first circuit (see Figure 3.3) consists of the following constituents:

- *Pyramid cells of the motor cortex (MotPyrC)*, which receive their inputs from higher cortical centers such as the associative center, and project to the motor neurons of spinal cord via the *pyramid track (PT)*
- A pathway from the pyramid track via the *red nucleus (RN)*, *inferior olive (IO)*, *nuclei pontis (NP)*, and *lateral reticular nucleus (LRN)* to the *pars intermedia of the cerebellum*

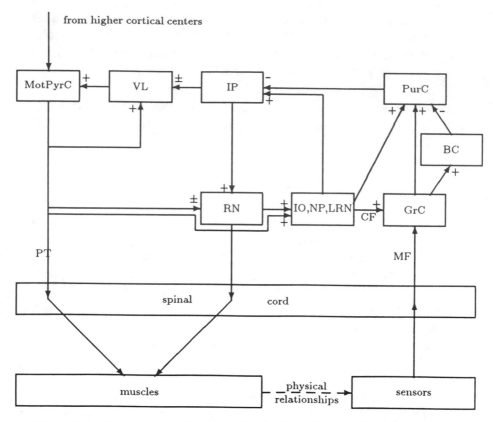

Figure 3.3. *Closed cerebellar loop. Connections denoted by (+) are excitatory, by (−) inhibitory. Those denoted by (±) are excitatory but with a parallel inhibitory connection within the successor component.*

- Massive excitatory and inhibitory "computations" in the pars intermedia (see Section 3.2.1) under the participation of *granule cells (GrC)*, *basket cells (BC)*, and *Purkinje cells (PurC)*
- Further excitatory and inhibitory processing in the *nucleus interpositus (IP)*
- A subsidiary motor pathway from the nucleus interpositus over the red nucleus and further via the *tractus rubrospinalis (RST)*
- Backprojection of the output from the nucleus interpositus via the *ventrolateral thalamus (VL)* to the pyramid cells of the motor cortex

- Physical relationships between muscle motion, environment, and sensors
- Transmission from sensors via the spinal cord and *mossy fibers* (*MF*) back to the granule cells of the cerebellum.

The most important loops in this scheme are:

1. The internal loop: pyramid cells → RN → IO, PN, LRN → cerebellum → IP → VL → pyramid cells
2. The external loop: pyramid cells → pyramid track → motor muscles → internal and external environment → mossy fibers → cerebellum → IP → VL → pyramid cells

The first loop is a correction loop. The rough output along the pyramidal track is corrected (and coordinated with other simultaneous movements) by information stored in the cerebellum. The latter loop is a genuine closed control loop, common in control theory. It is on the basis of the latter loop that Eccles refers to this structure as a "cerebellar closed-loop system."

Constituent parts of the second cerebellar circuit considered here are:

- The *pyramid cells of association cortex (AssPyrC)*, which project to the pyramid cells of the motor cortex (MotPyrC) of the former scheme
- A pathway from the pyramid track via the red nucleus (RN), inferior olive (IO), and nuclei pontis (NP) to the *cerebellar hemispheres*
- Massive excitatory and inhibitory computations in the cerebellar hemispheres
- Further excitatory and inhibitory processing in the *nucleus dentatus (DE)*
- Backprojection of the output from the nucleus dentatus via the ventrolateral thalamus (VL) to the pyramid cells of the association cortex.

This structure is obviously more linear than the previous one (see Figure 3.4). Although it contains an internal closed loop similar to the internal loop of the previous circuit, there is no environmental feedback. This is why it is basically an open-loop system.

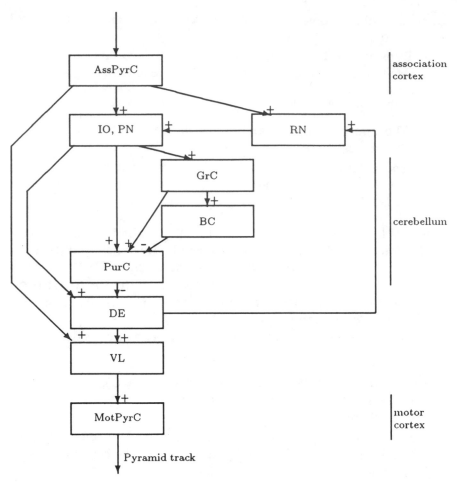

Figure 3.4. *Open cerebellar loop. Connections denoted by (+) are excitatory, by (−) inhibitory.*

Allen and Tsukahara [6] proposed an integration of both systems into a single motor information processing scheme (see Figure 3.5). The left column, corresponding to the cerebellar open-loop system, is assumed to be responsible for two tasks of motion control, for both of which an open-loop mode of operation is sufficient. The first of these is *motion planning*. Since planning takes place in advance, it cannot make use of sensory information about the result of motion. The other task is control of *preprogrammed motion*, that is, motion that is performed completely automatically, such as piano playing.

idea of desired motion

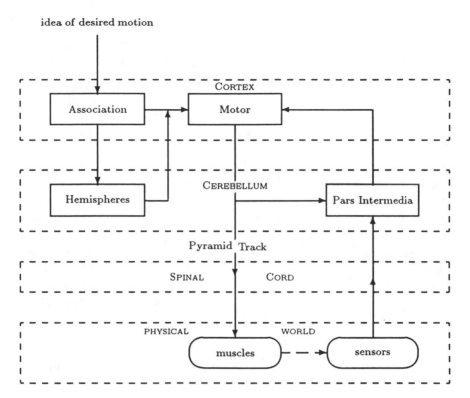

Figure 3.5. *Scheme of motor information processing. The left column represents the cerebellar open loop, the middle and the right columns, the cerebellar closed loop.*

Environmental feedback for such motion is not necessary. On the other hand, feedback is also impracticable in time-critical motion tasks; there is only enough time for the neuronal activations to follow the internal loop between pyramid cells and cerebellar hemispheres, which takes merely about 10 to 20 milliseconds.

The middle and right columns represent a cerebellar closed-loop system. This circuit performs both fast corrections via an internal loop and relatively slow (but reliable) corrections via an external, environmental loop. According to Allen and Tsukahara, this system is responsible for performing not completely automated motions. We can hypothesize that the motor cortex initiates motion on the voluntary level. Such completely voluntary movements are usually rather clumsy, slow, and imprecise, such as those observed in patients with cerebellar damage [29]. The correcting actions of the cerebellum take place if the situation is not completely novel or if there is a considerable nonvoluntary component. It is the cooperation of both systems that makes human motion control so precise, flexible, and adaptive.

3.4.3 Processing Stages in the Hippocampus

It is certainly more difficult to find complete evidence for complex high-level functions such as learning, associative memory, and selective data compression. This is why theories concerning circuits for such functions are more speculative than those for simple loops such as the muscle contraction servomechanism. However, they are not only useful for determining fruitful future directions of research, but also arise in close interaction with theories concerning abstract, artificial neural networks. An example of such theory is the model of information processing in the hippocampus proposed by Rolls [135].

A very simplified view of the information flow in the hippocampus is the following:

1. The hippocampus receives input from the *neocortex* (via the entorhinal cortex and perforant path).
2. This input enters a population of about 10^6 *dentate granule cells*.
3. *Mossy fibers* transmit the information from the granule cells to about 0.18×10^6 *pyramidal cells* in the *regio inferior* (*CA3*) (Cajal [21]).
4. The CA3 pyramidal cells project to the *CA1 pyramidal cells* (*regio superior* of Cajal [21]).
5. The output from the hippocampus goes from the CA1 cells over the entorhinal cortex back to the neocortex.

A flow diagram is given in Figure 3.6.

The arrangement of granule cells and their connections suggests the presence of the principle of competition (see Section 3.3.2) and application of the theory of *competitive learning* (Grossberg [51] and Kohonen [91]; see also Chapter 6). One of fundamental properties of the competitive model is that its output patterns are more orthogonal than its input patterns. This makes them more suitable as

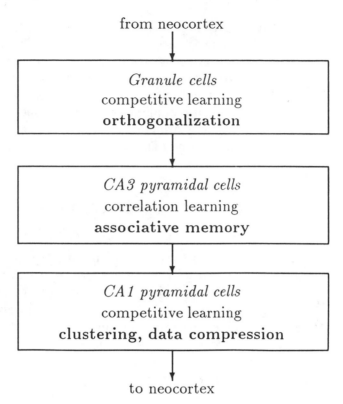

from neocortex

Granule cells
competitive learning
orthogonalization

CA3 pyramidal cells
correlation learning
associative memory

CA1 pyramidal cells
competitive learning
clustering, data compression

to neocortex

Figure 3.6. *Information-processing stages in hippocampus. Cell populations (italic), learning models, and information-processing functions (boldface).*

an input to linear pattern classifiers and linear associative memories (see Kohonen [91] and Chapter 6).

It is exactly this property that is utilized in the next stage of Rolls's model. This stage consists of CA3 pyramidal cells with extensive lateral connections and is supposed to work as an associative memory. The learning model may be correlation learning (Hebb [61]). This learning model has the capability of storing patterns and retrieving them by incomplete specifications (e.g., a part of the pattern or its distorted form). Kohonen [91] has shown that the performance of an associative memory is better for orthogonal patterns. So the previous competitive stage represents a useful preprocessing module.

The last stage of this process, consisting of CA1 pyramidal cells, has to do with *representational economy*. Rolls postulates, once more, competitive learning in this region. At this stage, the principal effect of competitive learning is proposed to be clustering, or data compression. Data input converging from various brain regions and sensory modalities can be viewed as conjunctions of many partial patterns. The data-compressing function of the CA1 module consists of identifying those parts of the conjunctive pattern space in which important pattern combinations are concentrated and then mapping these parts in an economical way. (This property of the competitive model is discussed in Chapter 6.)

3.5 INFORMATION-THEORETIC VIEW OF BRAIN PROCESSING

So far, we have addressed structural and qualitative aspects of brain information processing. Clearly, it is knowledge of structure that is crucial for designing artificial systems. On the other side, quantitative aspects of information processing are also important. They give us an idea about the magnitude of the task and thus feedback information about how far we may be from the ultimate goal of completely modeling the human brain.

The discipline concerned with quantitative aspects of information processing is information theory. Two fundamental concepts of information theory are *information* and *coding*. The concept of information can be explained informally in the following way. Suppose that there are two subjects communicating by means of a certain *alphabet*, consisting of a set of *symbols*. The communication takes place by sending symbols one by one from one subject to another. The information transmitted by one symbol is assumed to be higher if the symbol is scarce or unexpected. Quantitatively, it is equal to the binary logarithm of "scarcity" of symbol X measured as a reciprocal value of its probability $p(X)$:

$$\log_2 \frac{1}{p(X)}. \tag{3.1}$$

The average information of one symbol is then

$$\sum_i p(X_i) \log_2 \frac{1}{p(X_i)}, \tag{3.2}$$

summing over all symbols of the alphabet. The unit of information is a *bit*.

If the probabilities of symbols are modified by preceding symbol X_k, that is, if expectations are modified, *conditional information* can be computed by analogical formulas, using conditional probabilities $p(X_i \mid X_k)$:

$$\sum_k p(X_k) \sum_i p(X_i \mid X_k) \log_2 \frac{1}{p(X_i \mid X_k)}, \qquad (3.3)$$

summing additionally over all instances X_k of the preceding symbol. Conditional information is always lower than unconditional information. This is what we expect by common sense: Taking into account the information contained in the preceding symbols, we are probably less surprised by the present symbol. Consequently, the present symbol has a lower information content than it would have without considering the preceding symbol.

Average information per symbol after formula (3.2) for a given number of symbols is maximal if all symbols appear with equal probability. If the probabilities of individual symbols are very different, the information transmitted per symbol is low. We then speak of inefficient *coding*. Coding can be made efficient by transforming into another coding in which symbols of the original alphabet are mapped on symbol sequences of the new alphabet. Scarce symbols are translated to longer sequences, and frequent symbols to shorter sequences. More precisely, the length of this sequence should be, as closely as possible, proportional to the scarcity given by formula (3.1). An exact proportionality corresponds to *optimal coding*.

3.5.1 Information Streams in the Human Brain

Information measure (3.1) has been used by several researchers to evaluate information quantities in various processing phases in the human brain. In the following paragraphs, estimates of such quantities are given for sensory inputs, motor outputs, short-term memory, and long-term memory.

3.5.1.1 Sensory Inputs. In the human body there are about 10^9 receptors (Reichardt [129]). MacKay and McCulloch [104] estimated the transmission rate of a synapse at about 100 bits per second. Since the information from each receptor is conveyed over a synapse, the upper limit of the information capacity of all receptors per second is about $100 \times 10^9 = 10^{11}$ bits per second.

Frank [38] estimated the channel capacities of the individual cortex projection centers as:

- 10^7 bits per second (bps) for the optical channel
- 1.5×10^6 bps for the acoustic channel
- 0.4×10^6 bps for the tactile channel
- 15 to 46 bps for the olfactory channel
- 13 bps for the gustative channel

Obviously, visual information constitutes about 80% of the total capacity. This results in a total perceptive capacity of receptive fields on the order of magnitude of 10^7.

3.5.1.2 Motor Outputs. Motor information flow consists of sending commands from motor cortex projection centers and spinal cord reflex circuits to muscle innervation. An estimate of the channel capacity of this transmission is 3×10^6 bps. This capacity is distributed over all body regions. Individual muscles participate in this capacity proportionally to the functional requirements on the movements (e.g., precision) rather than to their size. A rough estimate of basic proportions is (Frank [37]):

- 32% for skeleton muscles
- 26% for hand
- 23% for speech
- 19% for face

3.5.1.3 Short-Term Memory. In Chapter 2 the term "short-term memory" was used in the normal sense in artificial neural network research: as a state of activation of processing units. Psychologists used this term in a slightly different (although probably strongly overlapping) sense: a memory in which observations or ideas that have become conscious remain for some time. Based on psychological experiments, this time has been estimated as approximately 10 seconds.

Miller, Brunner, and Postman [108] have experimented with learning letter sequences. Human subjects were requested to write the sequences down after their presentation. Curves have been received expressing the dependence of remembered information from the time of exposition, from which Frank [37] inferred that the maximum rate of information storage in the short-term memory is about 16 bits per second. Taking into account the temporal extension of short-term memory of about 10 seconds, the total capacity can be assessed to be approximately 160 bits.

3.5.1.4 Long-Term Memory.

The capacity of long-term memory is much more difficult to determine. An obvious reason for this is that in contrast to short-term memory, we cannot scan or write down its complete contents: first, for its huge volume, and second, for its unavailability to deliberate access.

An estimate of the information flow into long-term memory (the rate of storing) has been made by Aborn and Rubenstein [1]. Based on experiments with memorizing syllables, they came to a rate of 0.7 bit per second. Frank [37] has attempted to determine the total capacity of long-term memory indirectly by modeling the flow of learning and forgetting. His result has been a total capacity of order of magnitude 10^6 bits.

3.5.2 Some General Principles

Various experimental findings can be summarized into general principles and hypotheses. Two examples are presented next: optimal representation and data compression.

3.5.2.1 Hypothesis of Optimal Representation.

Howes and Solomon [71] made experiments concerning presentation times necessary to recognize words with various probabilities of appearance. It turned out that for scarce words these times are longer than for frequent words. Moreover, the time has been shown to be approximately proportional to the logarithm of scarcity of the word W:

$$\log_2 \frac{1}{p(W)}. \tag{3.4}$$

A comparison with formula (3.1) lead to the conclusion that the times are proportional to the information content of the word. If we recall the concept of optimal coding and assume that the time necessary to recognize a word is in some way proportional to the length of the sequence of some internal coding (e.g., by a sequence of neuron firings), a hypothesis is suggested that this coding is very close to the optimal coding. Further support for this hypothesis is given by Frank [37].

3.5.2.2 Data Compression. Let us recall the estimates of magnitudes of information flow in various phases of human information processing:

- 10^{11} bps for sensory inputs
- 10^7 bps for sensory projection areas
- 16 bps for input into short-term memory or "input into consciousness"

This sequence makes it clear that enormous data compression takes place. Compression of sensory data is probably performed in the thalamus (see Section 3.1.2). Another brain region that has been identified as participating in data compression is the hippocampus (Section 3.4.3). Finally, we can assume that *concept hierarchies* are the most powerful compression tool. They make it possible to describe a complex situation by a relatively short set of *supersymbols*: for example, words of a language.

PART II

Modular Learning

CHAPTER 4 ────────────────

Decomposition of Learning into Unsupervised and Supervised Learning

4.1 LEARNING ARCHITECTURE

The human way to learn mappings is incremental. Very approximately, we can recognize two successive stages of learning:

1. In the first stage, the environment is observed and the neural system tries to organize the huge number of sensory inputs in a less voluminous representation. There are a great variety of such organizing principles, but their common feature is that they transform sensory information to a form that makes subsequent supervised learning easier. An important point is that at this stage, the learning is relatively independent of the concrete situations in which the transformed information is used. It brings about overall facilitation of the subsequent learning tasks rather than being directly tailored to these tasks. A consequence of this is that there is a very loose feedback from the environment stating whether this organization is useful for individual cognitive tasks. The inherent optimizing criteria for these learning processes are, rather, focused on preserving the maximum sensory information or bringing sensory information into a form better suited for associative learning by simple learning principles such as the Hebbian rule. This loose feedback suggests an abstract learning model in which any external indicator of the correct response is

absent, the unsupervised learning model. Another widespread term for this is "self-organization." On a higher cognitive level, we would speak of "concept formation."

2. After an appropriate representation has been found in the self-organization stage, the usual supervised learning (i.e., learning with knowledge of desired mapping outputs) can be applied. Moreover, since the representation found in the self-organization phase possesses a certain universality (see item 1) it can be used for several supervised learning tasks.

Note 4.1.1 Throughout this book, the terms "unsupervised learning" and "self-organization" are considered to be synonymous.

The simplest neural network version of such a modular architecture is presented in Figure 4.1. A single-layer feature-discovery module receives the raw input and extracts a set of features from it. The feature representation of the input is then passed to the supervised learning module, which learns the desired associations. The latter module will mostly require a hidden layer to provide for the capability to represent nonlinear mappings.

Note 4.1.2 The architecture of Figure 4.1 is closely related to some classical pattern-recognition approaches based on feature extraction. One important class of such approaches uses the Karhunen–Loewe expansion, or principal components analysis (see, e.g., Devijver and Kittler [26, Chap. 9]). Another class is based on clustering algorithms (e.g., [26, Chap. 11]). Either Karhunen–Loewe expansion or clustering then plays the role of *task-independent* feature extraction, represented by the bottom box of Figure 4.1. By contrast, the underlying philosophy is different from that of approaches using *dedicated* features, such as amplitude histograms or power density coefficients (see, e.g., Harris and Ledwidge [60]).

4.2 EXISTING MODELS OF SELF-ORGANIZATION

In the search for principles of brain operation, several interesting self-organizing principles have been found. Most of them consist of two layers of neurons with unidirectional interaction between them.

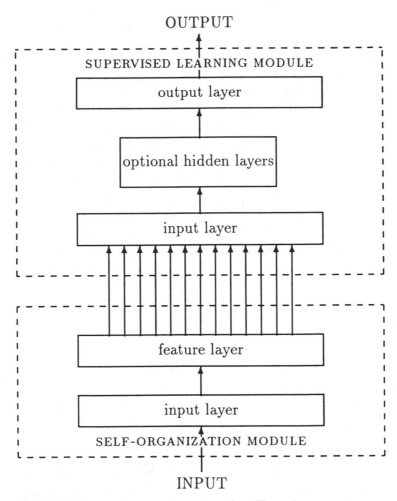

Figure 4.1. *Architecture for two-phase learning. There is a one-to-one correspondence between the feature layer of the self-organization module and the input layer of the supervised learning module.*

So a typical topology of the corresponding neural network models is a feedforward network with an input layer and a self-organizing feature layer. Although there is a great abundance of individual models, the bulk of them can be assigned to one of the following groups.

Competitive Model. This model is based on the competitive learning rule, studied by Grossberg (see, e.g., [48]; also Sections 2.5.5 and

7.5). A simpler competitive rule has been proposed by Rumelhart and Zipser [141]. Closely related are the feature maps of Kohonen [91]. The basic principle is that a unit of the feature layer is activated only if its input is larger than the input of all other feature units. Since the feature unit input can be viewed as a measure of similarity between the input pattern and the feature weight vector, the result of the competition is an exhaustive partitioning of the input pattern space into regions. Each of these regions is assigned to a feature unit. The weight vector of this feature unit corresponds primarily to the centroid of this region or an approximation of it. For a given set of input patterns, each of these regions defines a pattern *cluster*, a pattern subset whose intercluster variance is substantially higher than their intracluster variance. This group of models can be viewed as the neural network counterparts of the conceptual clustering of Stepp and Michalski [153] or the hybrid model of Lebowitz [98]).

In addition to the cluster interpretation, the result of the competitive model can be viewed as a quantization of continuous inputs (see Kohonen [91]). The quantization consists simply of applying the cluster membership functions to the input patterns. Each input pattern is mapped to a vector of the values of such membership functions. Since the clusters are exclusive (a consequence of the competitive activation rule), this vector is a unity vector. The activation domains of individual units (i.e., the subset of the input space in which the unit wins) have two interesting properties:

1. They cover only the part of the input space in which actual input patterns are concentrated (see Kohonen et al. [92]).
2. The density of weight vectors is, in some important cases, a monotonic function of the probability density on the input space (see [91] or Ritter and Schulten [132]); the units represent a model of input density.

Topology-Preserving Maps. If a neighborhood structure is defined on the second layer, and the competitive learning model is modified so that not only the winning unit but also its neighbors learn, this layer self-organizes itself into a topology-preserving mapping of the input (see Kohonen [91]). By "topology-preserving mapping" is meant that patterns that are neighbors in the input space are mapped to neighboring clusters in the cluster space. However, the extent to which this property is present depends on the dimensions of the input and feature spaces.

Self-Organization to Visual Features. Several models of self-organization are specialized to form feature extractors in early visual processing. An example is the self-organization of orientation-sensitive cells in the striated cortex (see von der Malsburg [105]). It is characteristic of these models that they learn features that do not vary very extensively from organism to organism. They are a part of the evolutionary process of the neural system rather than a specific reaction to the environment.

Principal Components Extraction. If a Hebbian learning rule with simultaneous weight norming is applied, the weight vector for a second-layer unit converges to the first principal component of the input, or the dominant eigenvector of the input correlation matrix (see Oja [114] or Linsker [103]). Since the first principal component has the important property of preserving the maximum amount of input variance, this self-organizing principle can be viewed as a procedure for data compression or optimal encoding into a single scalar value (corresponding to activation of the second-layer unit).

There are (at least) two possible approaches to using self-organization for facilitating supervised learning. First, we can extract some significant features out of the input data. Each feature will substitute a group of inputs. Such features will represent a certain data compression—instead of a high-dimensional sensory input, we consider a feature vector of a lower dimension. The goal of such a feature extraction can be some kind of optimal coding. Only the principal component extraction model satisfies the requirements concerning dimensionality reduction and optimal coding. This is why it is described in more detail in the next section. It will become a basis for more powerful feature-discovery principles: backward inhibition and delta-rule self-organization.

Second, we can preprocess the input to make it more tractable for simpler supervised learning algorithms. One possibility of doing so is to quantize the input by a competitive learning rule. It can be shown that such preprocessing substantially extends the class of mappings that can be represented by a single-layer network with linear units. In other words, by quantization, nonlinear mapping problems can be transformed to linear mapping problems. This is a great advantage from both the theoretical and practical viewpoints. Learning algorithms for linear mapping problems exhibit advantageous properties missing with nonlinear algorithms: guaranteed convergence and high convergence speed. Using competitive learning to preprocess input is discussed in Chapter 6.

CHAPTER 5

Supporting Supervised Learning by Feature Extraction

This chapter is concerned with the first group of self-organizing principles that have a potential for facilitating supervised learning. The general architecture for this learning task decomposition was given in Chapter 4 (Figure 4.1).

The role of the feature-discovery module is to transform the original input into a feature representation. This representation should in some way be simpler than the original one. The following properties of the feature representation appear desirable:

- The dimensionality of feature representation should be substantially lower than that of the original representation.
- The feature should represent an optimal coding of input (minimum information loss).

These are typical properties of human concepts based on super-symbols (Frank [37]): We are frequently able to describe a scene, originally represented by a vast number of retinal stimuli, by a couple of simple descriptive statements (dimensionality reduction), losing hardly any information relevant for further information processing (optimal coding; see Section 3.5).

Reducing the dimensionality brings about a twofold benefit. First, fewer weights are to be learned, and therefore the computational expense for learning is lower. Second, positive effects on the generalization capabilities of the model can be expected since generalization capabilities of a classifier are increasing with a decreasing number of free parameters. (This problem is treated in depth, for example, by Vapnik and Chervonenkis [159], Abu-Mostafa [2], Anshelevich et al. [8], Baum and Haussler [15], and Haussler [56]. Algorithms for reducing the number of free parameters have been proposed, for example, by Ji, Snapp, and Psaltis [54].)

5.1 NEURAL NETWORK FEATURE-DISCOVERY PRINCIPLES

5.1.1 Adaptive Rule of Oja

Oja [114] discovered a simple modification of the correlation learning rule (Hebb [61]) with interesting properties. The feature-discovery approaches of this chapter are generalizations of this rule, referred to further as the basic adaptive model. A similar adaptive rule has been studied by Kohonen [91].

The network architecture for the basic adaptive rule is shown in Figure 5.1. It is a single-layer network architecture with a single node in the feature layer and all input nodes connected with this feature node. Feature y is described by the vector $\mathbf{w}$ of weights assigned to connections to a feature node. The activation level of the feature

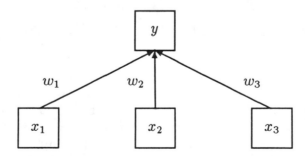

Figure 5.1. *Basic adaptive model.* $x_{1,2,3}$, *input units;* y, *feature units;* $w_{1,2,3}$, *weights.*

node is given by the following activation rule:

$$y = \mathbf{w}^T\mathbf{x}, \tag{5.1}$$

$\mathbf{x}$ being the input vector.

The continuous form of Oja's adaptive rule is

$$d\mathbf{w} = a\,y\mathbf{x}\,dt,$$

with $a \ll 1$ a constant.

The modification consists of keeping the weights normed: After each learning step, the weight vector is divided by its norm,

$$|\mathbf{w}| = \sqrt{\mathbf{w}^T\mathbf{w}}.$$

The complete learning rule is then

$$\mathbf{w} + d\mathbf{w} = \frac{\mathbf{w} + a\,y\mathbf{x}\,dt}{|\mathbf{w} + a\,y\mathbf{x}\,dt|}$$

$$= \frac{\mathbf{w} + a\,y\mathbf{x}\,dt}{\sqrt{1 + 2a\,y\mathbf{x}^T\mathbf{w}\,dt + a^2y^2\mathbf{x}^T\mathbf{x}(dt)^2}}. \tag{5.2}$$

By Taylor expansion of

$$\frac{1}{\sqrt{1 + 2a\,y\mathbf{x}^T\mathbf{w}\,dt + a^2y^2\mathbf{x}^T\mathbf{x}(dt)^2}},$$

leaving out all terms with a power of dt higher than 1, we get

$$\mathbf{w} + d\mathbf{w} = (\mathbf{w} + a\,y\mathbf{x}\,dt)(1 - a\,y\mathbf{x}^T\mathbf{w}\,dt)$$

$$= \mathbf{w} + a\,y\mathbf{x}\,dt - a\,y^2\mathbf{w}\,dt \tag{5.3}$$

or

$$d\mathbf{w} = a\,y\mathbf{x}\,dt - a\,y^2\mathbf{w}\,dt. \tag{5.4}$$

The weight vector $\mathbf{w}$ converges to the first principal component of input, that is, to the dominant eigenvector of the input correlation matrix

$$E[\mathbf{xx}^T].$$

For a proof, see Oja [114]. It is a special case of a more general theorem proven by Hrycej [75, 76]; see also Theorem 5.5.1 below.

If there were multiple feature nodes in the feature layer instead of a single one, the convergence of weights with the basic adaptive rule would apply to all of them. Since the state to which the weights converge is independent of initial weights, all feature unit weight vectors would converge uniformly to the same vector. In other words, all feature units would discover the same feature.

This makes clear that the basic adaptive model in its raw form is not a serious candidate for discovery of features that would support supervised learning. However, it can be modified in several ways to perform more satisfactorily. Two such modifications are proposed in the next two sections.

5.1.2 Backward Inhibition

The basic adaptive rule has been shown to have the property of learning the dominant eigenvector of the input correlation matrix. The dominant eigenvector is the eigenvector corresponding to the eigenvalue with the largest absolute value. It can obviously be interpreted as the strongest feature of input data. Although input data certainly contain other, weaker features, too, the learning rule is the most strongly attracted to the strongest feature. We can say that strong features are, in some way, overshadowing weak features.

Obviously, more subtle features can be discovered only if strong features overshadowing them are suppressed, or filtered out, in some way. This idea has been used in the backward inhibition learning algorithm of this section (see also Hrycej [72–74]). This algorithm consists of learning strong features and subsequently, filtering them from the input. The filtering is done by isolating the component orthogonal to the feature suppressed.

Let us now describe the procedure more formally. Suppose that a strong feature y_j has been learned successfully. Then the orthogonal projection of input vector $\mathbf{x}$ on the feature weight vector $\mathbf{w}_j$ is subtracted from $\mathbf{x}$. In this way the feature y_j is filtered out from the input $\mathbf{x}$. Since the feature to be suppressed is represented by the weight vector $\mathbf{w}_j$ with

$$|\mathbf{w}_j| = 1,$$

we get a modified input

$$\mathbf{x}_0 = \mathbf{x} - \frac{\mathbf{w}_j^T \mathbf{x}}{|\mathbf{w}_j|}\mathbf{w}_j$$

$$= \mathbf{x} - y_j\mathbf{w}_j \tag{5.5}$$

with $\mathbf{x}$ the original input, $\mathbf{x}_0$ the corrected input, and y_j the feature. The suppressed feature unit will not be activated further, since the modified feature activation is

$$y_{0j} = \mathbf{x}_0^T \mathbf{w}_j$$

$$= \mathbf{x}^T\mathbf{w}_j - y_j\mathbf{w}_j^T\mathbf{w}_j$$

$$= y_j - y_j|\mathbf{w}_j|$$

$$= 0.$$

The suppression can be simulated by propagating an inhibitory signal (in the size of feature activation) backward to input units. For example, if feature node A has been activated to activation level 2 via connections of strengths 0.5 and 0.3 to input nodes B and C, respectively, it inhibits nodes B and C by amounts $-2 \times 0.5 = -1$ and $-2 \times 0.3 = 0.6$, respectively.

The backward inhibition procedure is illustrated in Figure 5.2. Suppose that the feature y_1 (generally, the strongest k features y_1 to y_k) has already been learned and that its weights represent an already discovered eigenvector. A learning iteration for discovering feature y_2 [generally, the $(k + 1)$st feature y_{k+1}] consists of three steps:

1. Activation of feature y_1 by forward propagation over the weight vector $\mathbf{w}_1$ using the activation rule (5.1).
2. Backward inhibition by sending inhibitory signal of the magnitude $-y_1$ back over the weight vector $\mathbf{w}_1$ to the input, and sub-

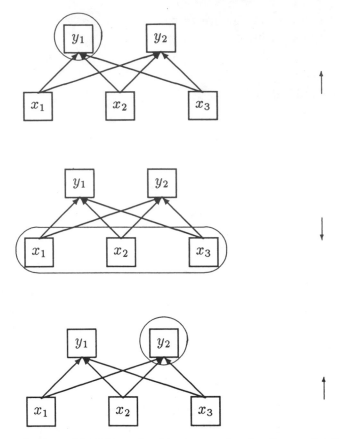

Figure 5.2. *Backward inhibition algorithm.* $x_{1,2,3}$, *input units;* y_1, *the first (dominant) feature unit;* y_2, *the second (weaker) feature unit. Arrows represent the direction of propagation in each phase. The nodes activated in the phase are encircled.*

tracting the resulting inhibitory values from the original input. This corresponds to the application of the backward inhibition rule (5.5). In this way the first feature is removed from the input.

3. Learning the weights of feature node y_2 by applying basic adaptive rule (5.3) to the modified input $\mathbf{x}_0$. This is done by activating the feature y_2 by the activation rule (5.1) using the modified input. Then learning takes place by the rule (5.3).

It is obvious from formula (5.5) that the backward inhibition algorithm corresponds directly to principal components analysis or the Karhunen–Loewe transform. After n features have been learned, the matrix **W** is equal to the matrix **U** such that each row of **U** is an eigenvector w_i of the input correlation matrix **C**:

$$\mathbf{U} = \begin{bmatrix} w_1^T \\ w_2^T \\ \vdots \\ w_n^T \end{bmatrix}.$$

The forward pass corresponds to the transformation $\mathbf{y} = \mathbf{U}\mathbf{x}$, that is, to the transformation of the input into the space defined by its n largest principal components. So we can say that the backward inhibition algorithm is a neural network implementation of principal components analysis.

Features found by backward inhibition frequently represent an implicit hierarchy (see Hrycej [76]). In this hierarchy, patterns are first partitioned according to the values of strong features and then subpartitioned by weaker features. This may be helpful in facilitating associative learning. Some associations can depend only on a single strong feature. Further associations may be encoded by a feature pair: the strong feature together with a weaker feature. Yet additional special features are then represented by adding further features, so that the actual encoding corresponds to a path in the hierarchy tree.

5.1.3 Delta-Rule Self-Organization

The backward inhibition learning rule of the preceding section has several advantageous properties, such as correspondence to principal components analysis and excellent convergence properties. On the other hand, its major shortcoming is its *sequentiality*. This property is a logical consequence of the principle of successive discovery of features in descending order of their strength.

However, it is certainly conceivable to look for other feature sets of approximately the same strength of individual features. Such features could then be found in parallel. Conversely, the balanced strength of individual features could be a *consequence* of the parallel feature discovery. This is reached by another generalization of the basic adaptive model (5.3), called delta-rule self-organization (Hrycej [75, 76]), which is the topic of this section.

The basic adaptive rule (5.3) can be rewritten as

$$dw = ay(x - yw)dt.$$

We can observe the delta-rule form of its right-hand side, containing the difference between the original x and its estimate $y = w$. This reminds of the widespread delta rule (Widrow and Hoff [170]), with x and y interchanged.

It is our goal to receive a whole feature vector y instead of a single feature y. This is exactly what the generalization consists of. The activation of the feature layer is described by the equation

$$y = Wx,$$

W being an $n \times m$ matrix of weights. The learning rule is generalized in a straightforward way:

$$dW = ay(x^T - y^T W)dt. \tag{5.6}$$

This corresponds to a weight modification in the direction of the derivative of quadratic error of the estimate of x by Wy:

$$e = (x - Wy)^2. \tag{5.7}$$

The dynamics of learning with the rule (5.6) is described by the following theorem.

Theorem 5.5.1   With the learning rule (5.6) and input x of dimension m with correlation matrix C (with distinct eigenvectors) applied to the first layer of a two-layer network, the $n \times m$ matrix W of weights between the first and second layers converges to a stable state

$$W = TU, \tag{5.8}$$

with $\mathbf{T}$ an arbitrary $n \times n$ orthonormal matrix and $\mathbf{U}$ a $n \times m$ matrix whose rows are n distinct eigenvectors corresponding to the n largest eigenvalues of $\mathbf{C}$.

Proof. The learning rule (5.6) can obviously be written as

$$d\mathbf{W} = a(\mathbf{W}\mathbf{x}\mathbf{x}^{\mathrm{T}} - \mathbf{W}\mathbf{x}\mathbf{x}^{\mathrm{T}}\mathbf{W}^{\mathrm{T}}\mathbf{W})\,dt.$$

The mean value over the distribution of $\mathbf{x}$ of weight matrix $\mathbf{W}$ will remain stable under the following condition:

$$\mathbf{W}\mathbf{C} = \mathbf{W}\mathbf{C}\mathbf{W}^{\mathrm{T}}\mathbf{W} \tag{5.9}$$

with

$$\mathbf{C} = E[\mathbf{x}\mathbf{x}^{\mathrm{T}}]$$

being the correlation matrix of input $\mathbf{x}$.

There is no trivial solution of the form

$$\mathbf{I} = \mathbf{W}^{\mathrm{T}}\mathbf{W},$$

since the rank of the matrix $\mathbf{W}$ is less or equal to $n < m$, and so is the rank of the $m \times m$ matrix $\mathbf{W}^{\mathrm{T}}\mathbf{W}$.

Let us search for a $\mathbf{W}$ in the form

$$\mathbf{W} = \mathbf{T}\mathbf{U} \tag{5.10}$$

with $\mathbf{T}$ a regular $n \times n$ matrix and $\mathbf{U}$ an $n \times m$ matrix with the following properties:

1. $\mathbf{U}$ is such that

$$\mathbf{U}\mathbf{U}^{\mathrm{T}} = \mathbf{I} \tag{5.11}$$

2. There is a $n \times n$ matrix $\mathbf{L}$ such that

$$\mathbf{U}\mathbf{C} = \mathbf{L}\mathbf{U}. \tag{5.12}$$

The condition (5.12) is satisfied for **U** such that each row of **U** is an eigenvector w_i of **C**:

$$U = \begin{bmatrix} w_1^T \\ w_2^T \\ \vdots \\ w_n^T \end{bmatrix} \tag{5.13}$$

and **L** is a $n \times n$ diagonal matrix

$$L = \begin{bmatrix} \lambda_1 & 0 & \cdots & 0 \\ 0 & \lambda_2 & \cdots & 0 \\ \multicolumn{4}{c}{\dotfill} \\ 0 & 0 & \cdots & 0 \end{bmatrix} \tag{5.14}$$

with corresponding eigenvalues λ_i on the diagonal:

$$
\begin{aligned}
UC &= \begin{bmatrix} w_1^T \\ w_2^T \\ \vdots \\ w_n^T \end{bmatrix} C \\[2em]
&= \begin{bmatrix} w_1^T \lambda_1 \\ w_2^T \lambda_2 \\ \vdots \\ w_n^T \lambda_n \end{bmatrix} \\[2em]
&= \begin{bmatrix} \lambda_1 & 0 & \cdots & 0 \\ 0 & \lambda_2 & \cdots & 0 \\ \multicolumn{4}{c}{\dotfill} \\ 0 & 0 & \cdots & 0 \end{bmatrix} \begin{bmatrix} w_1^T \\ w_2^T \\ \vdots \\ w_n^T \end{bmatrix} \\[1em]
&= LU. \tag{5.15}
\end{aligned}
$$

For condition (5.11) to hold, the eigenvectors have to be distinct and normalized. Substituting (5.10) into (5.9), we get

$$\mathbf{TUC} = \mathbf{TUCU}^T\mathbf{T}^T\mathbf{TU} \tag{5.16}$$

With the help of (5.12) and (5.15), (5.16) can be rewritten as

$$\mathbf{TLU} = \mathbf{TLUU}^T\mathbf{T}^T\mathbf{TU}.$$

Taking into account the relationship (5.11), this equation holds for $\mathbf{T}$ such that

$$\mathbf{T}^T\mathbf{T} = \mathbf{I}. \tag{5.17}$$

However, not all solutions of the form (5.10) are stable. Suppose that one of the rows (e.g., the last row $\mathbf{u}$) of $\mathbf{U}$ is slightly modified in the direction of an eigenvector $\mathbf{v}^T$ of $\mathbf{C}$ that is different from all rows of $\mathbf{U}$:

$$\mathbf{W} = \mathbf{T}\begin{bmatrix} \mathbf{U}_0 \\ \mathbf{u}^T + h\mathbf{v}^T \end{bmatrix}$$

with h a small quantity such that all terms containing its powers higher than 1 can be omitted, and $\mathbf{U}_0$ the matrix of the first $n - 1$ rows of $\mathbf{U}$.

An estimate of $\mathbf{x}$ and its derivative with regard to h can then be written in the following way:

$$z = \mathbf{W}^T y$$

$$= [\mathbf{U}_0^T \quad \mathbf{u} + h\mathbf{v}]\mathbf{T}^T\mathbf{T}\begin{bmatrix} \mathbf{U}_0 \\ \mathbf{U}^T + h\mathbf{v}^T \end{bmatrix}\mathbf{x}.$$

With the help of (5.17), this can be simplified to

$$z = [\mathbf{U}_0^T \quad \mathbf{u} + h\mathbf{v}]\begin{bmatrix} \mathbf{U}_0 \\ \mathbf{U}^T + h\mathbf{v}^T \end{bmatrix}\mathbf{x}$$

$$= [\mathbf{U}_0^T\mathbf{U}_0 + (\mathbf{u} + h\mathbf{v})(\mathbf{u}^T + h\mathbf{v}^T)]\mathbf{x}$$

$$= [\mathbf{U}_0^T\mathbf{U}_0 + \mathbf{u}\mathbf{u}^T + h(\mathbf{u}\mathbf{v}^T + \mathbf{v}\mathbf{u}^T) + h^2\mathbf{v}\mathbf{v}^T]\mathbf{x}.$$

Its derivative with regard to h is

$$\frac{d\mathbf{z}}{dh} = (\mathbf{uv}^T + \mathbf{vu}^T + 2h\mathbf{vv}^T)\mathbf{x}.$$

The derivative of the squared error e of the estimate $\mathbf{z}$ of input $\mathbf{x}$ with regard to h is, after discarding the term containing h^2,

$$\frac{de}{dh} = \frac{d\mathbf{z}^T}{dh}(\mathbf{z} - \mathbf{x})$$
$$= \mathbf{x}^T(\mathbf{uv}^T + \mathbf{vu}^T + 2h\mathbf{vv}^T)[\mathbf{U}_0^T\mathbf{U}_0 + \mathbf{uu}^T + h(\mathbf{uv}^T + \mathbf{vu}^T) - \mathbf{I}]\mathbf{x}.$$

Using the orthonormality of all rows of $\mathbf{U}_0$, $\mathbf{u}$ and $\mathbf{v}$, this can be simplified to

$$\frac{de}{dh} = \mathbf{x}^T[-\mathbf{uv}^T + h(\mathbf{uu}^T - \mathbf{vv}^T)]\mathbf{x}$$
$$= -\mathbf{x}^T\mathbf{uv}^T\mathbf{x} + h(\mathbf{x}^T\mathbf{uu}^T\mathbf{x} - \mathbf{x}^T\mathbf{vv}^T\mathbf{x})$$
$$= -\mathbf{u}^T\mathbf{xx}^T\mathbf{v} + h(\mathbf{u}^T\mathbf{xx}^T\mathbf{u} - \mathbf{v}^T\mathbf{xx}^T\mathbf{v}).$$

The mean value of the derivative of the squared error is

$$E\left[\frac{de}{dh}\right] = -\mathbf{x}^T\mathbf{Cv} + h(\mathbf{u}^T\mathbf{Cu} - \mathbf{v}^T\mathbf{Cv})$$
$$= -\lambda_u\mathbf{U}^T\mathbf{v} + h(\lambda_u\mathbf{u}^T\mathbf{u} - \lambda_v\mathbf{v}^T\mathbf{v})$$
$$= h(\lambda_u - \lambda_v). \tag{5.18}$$

with λ_u and λ_v being eigenvalues corresponding to the eigenvectors $\mathbf{u}$ and $\mathbf{v}$, respectively.

The relationship (5.18) describes the dependence of development of the weight matrix on the eigenvectors contained in the matrix $\mathbf{U}$. The gradient of the quadratic error (5.7) is negative if the eigenvalue λ_u (corresponding to the eigenvector $\mathbf{u}$ that is currently present in $\mathbf{U}$) is smaller that the eigenvalue λ_v (corresponding to the eigenvector $\mathbf{v}$ that is not present in $\mathbf{U}$). But this means that there is a direction of weight change for which the error decreases. Since the learning rule (5.5) is a gradient descent rule, any such solution is unstable.

In other words, the solution

$$W = TU$$

is stable only if there exists no eigenvector v of the input correlation matrix C not contained in U whose eigenvalue would be greater than the eigenvalue corresponding to some of the eigenvectors contained in U. This is the case only if U is composed of the eigenvectors corresponding to the n largest eigenvalues of C. Otherwise, an arbitrarily small perturbation h of the weights in the direction of the dominant eigenvector would suffice to make W be attracted to another solution. □

Note 5.1.1 Oja [115] has investigated the behavior of a different network with a feedback learning rule that is formally identical with the delta rule (5.6). Based on computational experiments, he conjectured the behavior postulated by Theorem 5.5.1, without a formal analysis.

The network implementation of this algorithm is similar to that of the backward inhibition algorithm. It consists of two phases (see Figure 5.3). In the first phase, the feature activations $y = Wx$ are computed. In the second phase the feature representation y is propagated backward over the same weight matrix W to compute the estimate $z = W^T y$ of the original input x. Learning consists of changing the weights proportionally to the difference $x - z$ according to rule (5.6).

Obviously, the transformation Ux corresponds to extracting n principal components of x. The matrix T represents an additional rotation of this transformation. For a more parallel but less stable implementation of the backward inhibition principle, and for a way that it can be used to enhance the competitive unsupervised learning, see Hrycej [72, 73].

5.1.4 Relationship Between Delta-Rule Self-Organization and Backward Inhibition

We have seen two generalizations of Oja's basic adaptive model: delta-rule self-organization and backward inhibition model. Both are

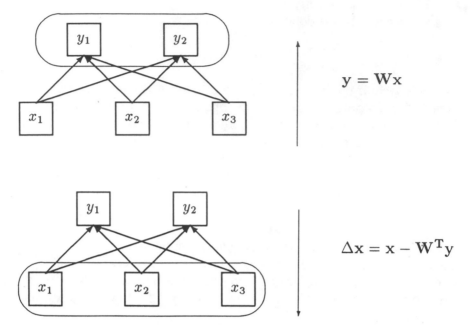

Figure 5.3. *Network for delta-rule self-organization. $x_{1,2,3}$, input units; $y_{1,2}$, output units. Arrows represent the direction of propagation in each phase. The nodes activated in the phase are encircled.*

related to principal components analysis. Even the similarity of the transformations materialized by both models, $y = Ux$ (backward inhibition) and $y = TUx$ (delta-rule self-organization), is striking. Both share the following properties:

1. The vector y preserves the maximum of the variance of x that can be preserved by any linear transformation of x into an n-dimensional vector y $(n < m)$. So the dimensionality of data can be reduced with a minimum loss of information. In a sense, y represents an optimal coding of x.

2. The vector $z = W^T y$ is an optimal estimate of the original vector x. This results from the fact that learning rule (5.6) can also be viewed as a gradient method of finding the minimum of the mean-squared error of this estimate. The minimum is reached exactly for the weight matrix W.

A comparative study of learning speed and accuracy of both models can be found in Hrycej [75]. Their data compression capabilities are compared with that of autoassociative multilayer networks with backpropagation learning. Both methods presented here are clearly superior to autoassociative networks. Further results can be summarized as follows:

1. Compared with the backward inhibition algorithm, the delta rule needs a larger number of iterations. This is due to its instability for large values of the learning rate, for which the backward inhibition model is still stable and converges rapidly (optimal values of a have been 1.0 for backward inhibition but 0.03 for the delta rule).

2. For a larger number of features (e.g. 20), this is traded off by the fact that an iteration of the backward inhibition model takes longer and its computing time scales with $O(n^2)$, whereas an iteration of the delta rule, such as that of the autoassociative perceptron, scales linearly.

3. On the other hand, delta-rule learning is incremental, which is especially important (a) if data compression is to be done for an input with continually changing statistical properties or (b) if the termination rule for the algorithm is defined in terms of the estimation accuracy. The computational expense can gradually be varied with the accuracy required for a particular application.

4. Delta-rule learning is completely parallel; all weights are learned simultaneously. This is not the case for the backward inhibition model, where higher principal components have to be found before lower ones can be found.

5. The features found by the backward inhibition algorithm correspond directly to the principal components. Consequently, their information contents may be very different, depending on the differences between corresponding eigenvalues. By contrast, the features found by delta-rule self-organization tend to be of balanced strength. The difference between the two is illustrated in Figures 5.4 and 5.5. The delta-rule features have approximately equal variances, whereas the backward inhibition variances may differ considerably. This is important if we want to limit this maximal error of the encoding/decoding procedure if some of the features get lost.

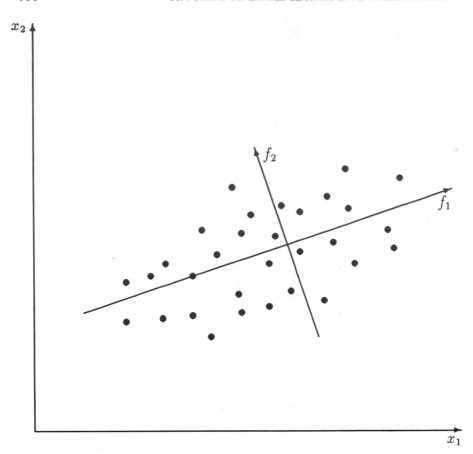

Figure 5.4. *Features found by backward inhibition.* f_1*, the strongest feature (the first principal component);* f_2*, weaker feature (the second principal component). Patterns in the input space are represented by filled circles.*

6. A consequence of the asymmetric distribution for backward inhibition is that very weak eigenvectors (i.e., those corresponding to very low eigenvalues) get lost in the remainders of
   stronger eigenvectors. For example, with 20 features, the twentieth eigenvector may be weaker than what remained from the
   dominant eigenvector because of limited computational accuracy. Consequently, a weak "echo" of the dominant eigenvector
   is discovered as the twentieth feature instead of the twentieth
   eigenvector. This is not the case for the delta rule, where all
   features tend to be of approximately the same strength.

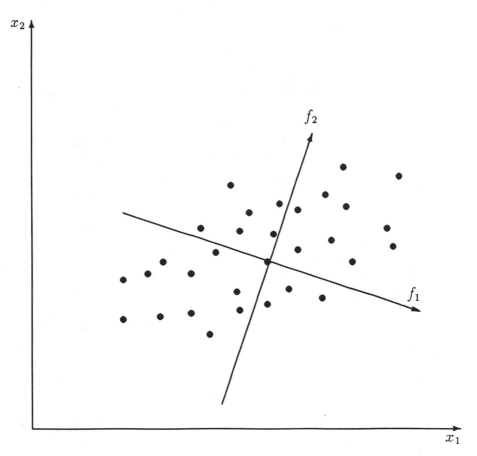

Figure 5.5. *Features found by delta-rule self-organization. $f_{1,2}$, two features of balanced strength. Patterns in the input space correspond to those of Figure 5.4.*

5.2 COMPUTATIONAL EXPERIENCE AND CONCLUSIONS

The hypothesis of previous sections that learning is more efficient with the feature representation than with the original input will now be verified by computational experiments.

5.2.1 Handwritten Digits

To evaluate the generalization capabilities of individual classifiers, the handwritten-digit classifiers have been trained by two different sets:

1. The original training set of 1000 samples of each digit (i.e., a total of 10,000 samples)
2. A reduced training set of 100 samples of each digit (i.e., a total of 1000 samples)

The latter set has been received by random sampling from the former set. In both cases, the same test set of 1000 samples of each digit (of course, different from the training set) has been taken.

The data have been compressed by delta-rule self-organization. (Backward inhibition feature discovery performed almost equivalently, but slightly worse than, delta-rule self-organization.) The compression has been to:

- 20 features, covering 70.9% of total variance
- 40 features, covering 80.4% of total variance.

The misclassification rates for linear classifiers are given in Tables 5.1 and 5.2 for backpropagation classifiers, with various numbers of hidden units in Tables 5.3 and 5.4.

Obvious conclusions from these results are:

1. Although the training set performance deteriorates for data compressed by feature extraction, the test set performance with

TABLE 5.1   Handwritten Digits: Misclassification Rates (Percent)[a]

	Noncompressed	20 Features	40 Features
Full set	1.29	6.00	3.56
Reduced set	0.00	3.50	0.00

[a]Linear classifiers, training set.

TABLE 5.2   Handwritten Digits: Misclassification Rates (Percent)[a]

	Noncompressed	20 Features	40 Features
Full set	5.55	6.31	5.08
Reduced set	14.70	8.83	9.35

[a]Linear classifiers, test set.

TABLE 5.3 Handwritten Digits: Misclassification Rates (Percent)[a]

	Hidden Units	Noncompressed	20 Features	40 Features
Full set	5	3.57	8.39	6.15
	10	0.04	3.27	1.93
	20	0.00	1.33	0.05
	40	0.00	0.78	0.01
Reduced set	5	0.00	4.60	0.80
	10	0.00	0.00	0.00
	20	0.00	0.00	0.00
	40	0.00	0.00	0.00

[a]Backpropagation classifiers, training set.

TABLE 5.4 Handwritten Digits: Misclassification Rates (Percent)[a]

	Hidden Units	Noncompressed	20 Features	40 Features
Full set	5	9.48	8.94	7.32
	10	5.35	4.35	4.14
	20	3.73	3.68	3.34
	40	2.53	3.36	2.77
Reduced set	5	17.36	12.86	12.57
	10	10.47	9.37	8.88
	20	8.53	8.90	8.00
	40	7.38	7.44	7.32

[a]Backpropagation classifiers, test set.

feature extraction is clearly superior (with a few insignificant exceptions).

2. The extent to which the classifiers using feature discovery perform better for the test set is significantly larger if the reduced training set is taken.

Both conclusions indicate *improved generalization with supervised learning supported by feature discovery*.

5.2.2 Thyroid Data

Some initial runs have been performed on low-cost hardware with limited performance. This is why for the first experiments only approximately a tenth of the data set—360 records from the 1985 set and 360 from the 1986 set—were randomly selected. The former set served as a training set, the later as a test set. I presented the results of these experiments in [76]. Data compression led to substantial improvement of generalization.

The results for the full thyroid data set were less satisfactory. With compressed data, the test set misclassification rates have never been below 3%. These results are significantly worse than those for non-compressed data. The reason for this seems to be obvious. As stated in Section 1.3.1, thyroid data represent a *highly nonlinear* classification problem. This can be seen by poor performance of linear discriminant analysis. Therefore, we can hardly expect a linear data compression transformation materialized by the backward inhibition of delta rule–based features to improve the performance.

Another reason is the fact that the 21 input variables of thyroid data are to a large extent independent and thus difficult to compress without significant information loss. This results in a low portion (72.6%) of the input variance that could be explained by as many as 10 out of 21 features. For five features, the figure is only 45.9%. This contrasts with the handwritten-digit data set, for which feature extraction has been remarkably helpful: For 20 and 40 features out of 256 input variables, the percentages of variance explained are 70.9% and 80.4%, respectively.

The following conclusions for the applicability of the modularization by feature extraction can be made:

1. *The classification problem should be one of limited nonlinearity.*
2. *The data input should exhibit significant dependencies.*

5.3 RELATED WORK

Profitable effects of data compression have frequently been observed in classical discriminant analysis. The most trivial form is a careful selection of input variables (see, e.g., Hocking [68]) using knowledge about causal relationships between the individual variables and object classes. A more formal approach is based on the widespread Karhunen–Loewe transform (e.g., Fu [39] or Fukunaga and Koontz [40]). This transform is used for compression of input into feature

vectors as well as for generation of orthogonal features. As shown
in the preceding sections, there is a close correspondence between
Karhunen–Loewe transform and neural network feature-discovery
models.

Feature extraction by autoassociative perceptron to facilitate associative learning has been proposed by Ballard [10]. His explicit goal
has been the reduction of computational complexity, in particular
better scaling for a growing number of hidden layers.

There have also been some investigations on the neural network
field concerned with preprocessing data by Karhunen–Loewe transform or principal components analysis. One of these investigations
is reported in the work of Vrckovnik, Carter, and Haykin [160] and
Vrckovnik, Chung, and Carter [161]. For the task of classification of
radar waveforms received from asphalt-covered bridge decks (with
the goal of identifying damages and their types), the original sample
of 140 input values has been reduced by principal components analysis to 15 features (corresponding to the first 15 principal components). On both data sets, the original and the compressed, a radial
basis network classifier has been applied. While the test set classification accuracy for the original data set has been 89.92%, the
corresponding result for the compressed data has been 99.15%. Feature extraction by the delta-rule self-organization has been applied to
a vowel recognition task by Leen, Rudnick, and Hammerstrom
[97]. They compressed 64 spectral components of speech samples
to various numbers (5 to 30) of features. Except for the five-fea-
ture trials, the compression generally improved, or at least did
not deteriorate significantly, the performance of the backpropagation classifier applied to the data. It has also been observed that
compressing the data allows a significant decrease in the number
of hidden units necessary to reach a certain classification performance.

There has also been some related work concerning the particular
topic of relationship between principal components analysis and various learning rules. Bourlard and Kamp [18] have studied the explicit
form of optimal coefficients for a three-layer autoassociate network.
For linear activation functions in both hidden and output layers, they
found a solution in the form (notation modified)

$$W_1 = SU \qquad (5.19)$$

and

$$\mathbf{W}_2 = \mathbf{U}\mathbf{S}^{-1}, \tag{5.20}$$

$\mathbf{W}_{1,2}$ being the weight matrices of hidden and output layers, respectively, $\mathbf{U}$ corresponding to definition (5.13), and $\mathbf{S}$ an arbitrary regular $n \times n$ matrix. There is obviously a close relationship to Theorem 5.1.1. Like the model presented here, a three-layer autoassociative network with linear activation functions and weights (5.19) and (5.20) performs optimal linear data compression and decompression, the compressed data being represented by activation of the hidden linear units. However, the hidden layer is in a rather arbitrary relationship with the principal components: The relationship is obscured by the arbitrary regular matrix $\mathbf{S}$, which can rescale and recombine the principal component vectors to any extent. By contrast, the representation found by the feature layer of the delta-rule self-organizing model is a rotation of the principal components (a consequence of the orthonormality of matrix $\mathbf{T}$).

If the coefficients are to be found by the backpropagation learning rule, $2mn$ coefficients have to be determined instead of mn coefficients of the delta-rule self-organization model. This seems to have a serious impact on the learning speed (see Hrycej [75]).

Bourlard and Kamp argue that using a linear activation function is *always* preferable to a nonlinear, (e.g., sigmoid) function. However, this statement must be somewhat restricted. Data compression by linear networks is optimal in the sense of a linear transformation, not in the information-theoretic sense. For example, the well-known encoder problem (see, e.g., Rumelhart et al. [139]) cannot be solved by any linear model, including, of course, delta-rule self-organization. On the other side, the argument of Bourlard and Kamp concerning the superiority of linear models in guaranteed convergence and learning speed is certainly valid and has been supported by the computational experiments of Hrycej [75].

An interesting approach that can be viewed as an attempt to overcome the linearity limitation is that of Sirat, Viala, and Remus [149]. It is closely related to the subspace algorithm of Oja and Kohonen [116]. They have used a set of competing three-layer linear perceptrons. Each data set is enclosed by the perceptron with the lowest square error. Each perceptron is thus assigned a certain subset of the input space. This model has been applied to image compression.

There have also been several proposals of networks whose structure is *dedicated* to principal components analysis (e.g., Rosenblatt et al. [137]).

5.4   FEATURE EXTRACTION NETWORK AS A LEARNING MODULE

The computational experiments of the preceding section confirm the hypothesis that feature extraction by backward inhibition or delta-rule self-organization is a helpful preprocessing stage for subsequent supervised learning if the task is not extremely nonlinear. So feature extraction can represent a learning module.

There are two measures that can be used as success criteria for the feature extraction module. The first criterion is based on the decomposition of the input variance, which is equal to the trace of the input correlation matrix, or

$$\sum_i \text{var}(x_i) \qquad (5.21)$$

with x_i the ith input variable. This variance can be decomposed into parts assigned to individual principal components (corresponding to the features or their rotations) of the correlation matrix. The quality of encoding input into the features can be measured by the proportion of the input variance explained by the features y_j. This measure can be written as

$$m_1 = \frac{\sum_j \text{var}(y_j)}{\sum_i \text{var}(x_i)}. \qquad (5.22)$$

If the measure m_1 is close to 1, the input is almost completely encoded into the features.

The second criterion is based on the fact that optimal features should guarantee an optimal reconstruction of the original input. In other words, the estimate of the original input **x** by the inverse transformation W^T of the feature vector **y** should be very close. A mean-squared error of this estimate is

$$m_2 = E\left[\sum_i \left(x_i - \sum_j w_{ji}y_j\right)^2\right]. \tag{5.23}$$

This measure gives us a picture of the precision of the encoding of input by the features discovered. For example, the mean-squared error of the estimate of pixel values in the handwritten-digit data set from 20 features is 215.04. So each of the 256 pixel values could be estimated with a deviation of $\sqrt{0.8} \doteq 0.9$. Since the gray values vary from 0 to 255, this estimate is certainly very good.

With these two measures, we are able to assess the success of feature discovery. If their values are not satisfactory, the following recommendations can be made:

- If the values of both measures are improving with further iterations, the learning process should be continued.
- If both measures reached stable values that cannot be improved by additional learning, the number of features should be increased.
- If the number of features has reached a significant percentage of the input dimensionality (e.g., 50%) and the values of both measures are still unacceptably low, the problem can be classified as highly nonlinear, and another modularization approach (e.g., the quantization approach of Chapter 6) should be attempted.

CHAPTER 6 ⎯⎯⎯⎯⎯⎯⎯⎯⎯⎯

Supporting Supervised Learning by Quantization

6.1 CASE FOR SINGLE-LAYER LEARNING PRINCIPLES

The decomposition of learning into a feature-discovery part and a supervised learning part discussed in Chapter 5 has been motivated by the intention to *reduce the size* of the supervised learning task, with the expectation that a smaller learning problem will be easier to solve.

The idea underlying the approach of this chapter is different. Here we try to *transform the learning task into an easier one*. More precisely, the goal is to make an originally nonlinear problem linear.

There is an interesting historical perspective for this approach. Since the critical paper of Minsky and Papert [110], it has been taken for granted that networks based on very simple principles, such as the single-layer perceptron, do not possess the computational power necessary for solving interesting problem classes. One of the most prominent results of the search for more sophisticated networks with more general capabilities has been the error back-propagation algorithm (Werbos [166] and Rumelhart et al. [139]). The networks trained by this algorithm seem to meet the research objectives. Feedforward networks with sigmoid units are in principle capable of modeling arbitrary continuous mappings, and numerous successful applications prove their feasibility. However, there are also some less satisfactory properties of the backpropagation model:

- Although the model frequently exhibits satisfactory results in practice, its *convergence is unreliable* and parameter sensitive. This contrasts with often very good (and mathematically proven) convergence of simpler, single-layer models.

- A frequently observed property is its *nonmonotonic generalization behavior*: A larger network, that is, a network with a larger number of hidden units, frequently performs worse than a simple one on the test data set, although its performs better on the training data set (see the experiments of Weiss and Kapouleas [165] and the theoretical analyses of Haussler [56], Anshelevich et al. [8], and others). In other words, a larger network may generalize more poorly. This is a serious drawback for practical applications, since test set performance, rather than training set performance, is the goal of classification. This property can be explained by the excessive expressiveness of large nets. The class of mappings they can represent is so large that there are many instantiations that conform with the training set, which reduces the probability that a specific instantiation closely fits the mapping from which the training set is a sample.

- The excessive expressiveness has one more harmful consequence. While the class of possible mappings is very broad, there are virtually no constraints concerning the *smoothness* of the mapping represented by the network. But smoothness constraints are the only means of enforcing generalization of the model (see Poggio and Girosi [128]) if there is no additional information about the nature of the mapping. A practical consequence is, once more, that an insufficiently smooth classifier may perform excellently on the training set but poorly on the test set. This is not the case for simple classifiers such as the perceptron; its linearity is itself a very strong smoothness constraint.

- As its authors admit [139], its *biological plausibility* is rather low. In particular, each cell must work in two different modes, depending on the propagation direction. (This aspect will not be pursued further in this work.)

These are some harmful properties that simple single-layer models do not share with the backpropagation model. We can view them as the cost of its improved computational power. But we can also pose the question if some weaker models are not sufficient for a broad class of problems and then possibly benefit from other advantageous properties of such weaker models. In particular, it is worth investigating if there are perhaps some synergies between various simple models that would relax some of the limitations of their power but still preserving their convergence reliability and inherent smoothness. Particularly interesting in the context of this work is the combination of supervised learning and self-organization.

It is clear that we can hardly expect the feature-discovery models of Chapter 5 to reduce the dimensionality and make the learning problem more linear simultaneously. This is why we shall try another single-layer self-organization model for preprocessing: the competitive learning model (Grossberg [48], Kohonen [91], or Rumelhart and Zipser [141]). This model performs clustering, or quantization of input.

So the learning decomposition principles pursued in this chapter leads to two learning modules:

1. A self-organizing quantization module
2. A linear, single-layer classifier, that is, a single-layer perceptron

To design an appropriate quantization module and to get an idea about the class of tasks that can be solved by a modular architecture of this type, some analysis of the computational power of single-layer perceptrons is necessary. Further, since there is no guarantee of convergence to a state with well-described characteristics for the competitive learning model, an optimal trade-off must be found between the simplification of the model and its convergence properties. These are the topics of the following section.

A further step toward an optimal use of single-layer networks is to find an optimal learning rule for them. It has been rather astonishing to find that widespread linear classifiers based on the mean-squared error (as well as the Widrow–Hoff rule equivalent to them) are far from being optimal for classification tasks. A linear model superior to them is given in Section 6.3. The results of computational experiments supporting the hypotheses of Sections 6.2 and 6.3 are presented in Section 6.4.

6.2 SUPPORTING SINGLE-LAYER PERCEPTRONS BY QUANTIZATION

A classical simple linear learning principle is the perceptron rule proposed by Rosenblatt [136]. This learning rule has been shown to be capable of finding the separating hyperplanes for linearly separable classes. The goal of this section is to discuss briefly:

1. The real impact of this limitation if the classes are defined by logical expressions
2. How the class of problems solvable by a linear classifier is extended if the input is quantized before classification

6.2.1 Perceptron and Boolean Features

It is a common assumption that linear classifiers, implemented by single-layer perceptrons, are too weak for reasoning. A frequently stated example is the logical XOR function. However, it is not obvious if XOR represents a very interesting class of problems. On the contrary, it seems to be rather untypical for human reasoning. While a vast number of concepts are defined in terms of conjunctions or disjunctions of simpler concepts, there are hardly real-world concepts that would be defined in terms of XOR (for more arguments against XOR, see Fahlman [35]). So let us first investigate which classes of logical functions can be materialized by single-layer perceptrons (Hrycej [83]).

First there are two trivial cases:

- Case 1: *conjunction*
- Case 2: *disjunction*

Although these trivial cases do not look very general at first glance, we have to realize that most human concepts are defined as pure conjunctions. For example, "bird" is "animal," "flying," and "feathered."

It is well known that any logical function can be expressed by means of conjunction, disjunction, and negation. The implementation of negation in a perceptron is trivial: the corresponding weight is simply set to -1, and the threshold of the output unit is diminished by 1. So we should investigate which subclasses of the positive-literal propositions can be mapped. One such subclass is such that in a conjunctive normal form:

- Case 3: *all disjuncts within a conjunct are exclusive.*

In this case, each conjunct contributes to the sum by either 1 (if one disjunct is true) or 0 (if no disjunct is true). So the entire proposition is true if the sum of all inputs is greater or equal to the number of conjuncts. For example, a "vehicle" is "two-wheeled," "three-wheeled," or "four-wheeled" and "motor-driven" or "animal-driven." This definition of "vehicle" has the structure $(a \lor b \lor c)\&(d \lor e)$: a, b, c as well as d, e being exclusive.

Another class is such that in a disjunctive normal form

- Case 4: *one conjunct implies all other conjuncts of the same disjunct.*

For example, given the proposition $(a \& b) \lor (c \& d)$ and $(a \rightarrow b)\&$ $(c \rightarrow d)$, $(a \& b)$ and $(a \rightarrow b)$ imply a and $(c \& d)$ and $(c \rightarrow d)$ imply c. So the entire proposition can be reduced to a pure disjunction $(a \lor c)$. Although b and d are redundant in the definition, expressions of this type are frequently used in commonsense expressions. It must be emphasized that the implication requirement (as well as the disjointness requirement) is relative to the "universe of discourse" of the classifier concerned. For example, "woman with red stockings" is a conjunction of this type (b representing "woman" and a, "with red stockings") if among the objects to be classified it can be expected that only women wear red stockings (i.e., $a \rightarrow b$), although men wearing red stockings may generally exist.

6.2.2 Quantization: Extending the Computational Power of Single-Layer Perceptrons for Continuous Features

We have seen that single-layer perceptrons possess considerable computational power for "everyday life" Boolean categories. Let us now turn to the case in which objects to be classified are described by continuous features instead of Boolean values. It is clear that taking continuous features directly would lead to the well-known limitation on linear separating hypersurfaces (i.e., hyperplanes). However, there are some simple preprocessing principles that relax this limitation. All of them can be viewed as some kind of quantization.

Direct n-Dimensional Quantization. One such principle is simply quantizing the n-dimensional input into an n-dimensional grid. The grid field into which a given combination of input values falls uniquely determines the function value (except for the accuracy limitation given by the grid density). Therefore, an arbitrary mapping can be expressed as a disjunction of the Boolean variables describing the membership of the given input in the individual grid fields. So a single-layer perceptron would be sufficient for classification (Case 2 of the preceding subsection). However, even a grid considering only two intervals for each input would produce a Boolean vector of length 2^n, a clearly unacceptable size for nontrivial input dimensionalities.

Optimized n-Dimensional Quantization. A way to optimize the quantization by deforming the grid to consider only existing input value combinations is the self-organization principle of Kohonen maps [91]. It has actually been used for classification [92], and good results have been reported for some tasks. However, if the input value combinations are distributed over a large part of the n-dimensional space, the margin for optimization shrinks, and the Kohonen map becomes too sparse a representation of the input. Additionally, during computational experiments convergence turned out not to be very reliable (on the other hand, some good convergence properties of self-organizing maps have been postulated by Erwin, Obermayer, and Schulten [33]).

Direct One-Dimensional Quantization. A less powerful but better scaling alternative is to quantize each individual input separately (Hrycej [83]). The n-dimensional input is then described by a qn-dimensional Boolean vector (q being the number of intervals into which the continuous values are partitioned). With this representation, the membership in a particular field of the n-dimensional grid is now represented by a conjunction of exactly n Boolean variables instead of a single variable. Consequently, an arbitrary mapping cannot generally be represented by a linear perceptron, since the logical

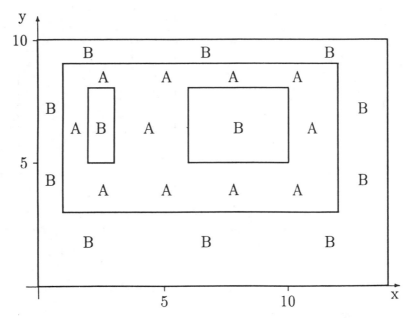

Figure 6.1. *Separability example. Although classes A and B are nonconvex and even discontinuous, they are separable by one-dimensional quantization (see the text).*

expression to be found is generally a disjunction of conjunctions. However, there is an interesting subclass of mappings that is within the scope of linear perceptrons. Since each variable has a value from exactly one interval at a time, we can make use of Case 3 of Section 6.2.1. This subclass is characterized by the requirement that the region for each function value is described by a conjunction of disjunctions composed of Boolean variables corresponding to a single input variable. In terms of input variables, these are expressions of the type $(1 < x < 2 \vee 3 < x < 6 \vee 10 < x < 12)\&(3 < y < 5 \vee 8 < y < 9)$. So the classifier of this type can separate the classes A (defined by this expression) and B given in Figure 6.1. Note that the *linear* classifier acquired, by means of preceding quantization, the capability of separating *nonconvex*, even *discontinuous* classes.

Optimized One-Dimensional Quantization. The interval representation can be optimized by self-organization to account for nonhomogeneous distribution of input values. This model can then be viewed

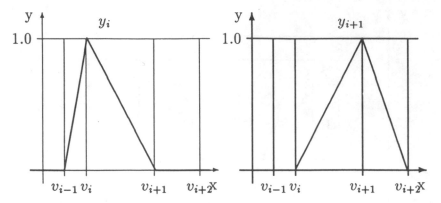

Figure 6.2. *"Fuzzy membership" activation functions. Left: activation function for the ith interval (centered about v_i); right: activation function for the $(i + 1)$st interval.*

as a set of Kohonen maps with a single input dimension (referred to further as "one-dimensional maps"). An outstanding feature of such maps (in contrast to the general case) is that their convergence to a density closely related to the probability density of the input has been proven (see Ritter and Schulten [132]). This also makes their optimizing effect obvious; they form narrower intervals in dense input regions and broader intervals in sparse regions.

With interval membership expressed by Boolean variables, all values falling into the same interval are represented in the same way, and the information about their position within the interval is completely lost. This information loss can be prevented by using "fuzzy membership" of the following form (see Figure 6.2). Each interval is represented by its center. For a given input x, the activation y_i of the cell with center v_i is

$$
y_i = \begin{cases} \dfrac{x - v_i}{y_i + 1 - y_i} & \text{for } x \geq v_i \\[2ex] \dfrac{v_i - x}{y_i - y_i - 1} & \text{for } x < v_i. \end{cases}
$$

This activation rule has the advantageous property that the sum of the activations of all quantizing cells y_i corresponding to an input value x (if y_1 and y_m are lower and upper bounds for x) is always equal to 1.

6.3 SUPERVISED LEARNING MODULE

In Section 6.2 a self-organization model transforming the input into a form that makes linear separability more probable has been presented. It has also been argued that the power of linear classifiers is frequently sufficient for recognizing concepts described by logical expressions of types used in real life.

To exploit the full potential of this modularization principle, we must also investigate which type of linear learning rule is optimal for classification. Optimality of the learning rule is closely connected with the objective function that is optimized during learning. Typically, an objective function for classification is an *error measure* to be minimized.

The best known learning models, such as the Widrow–Hoff rule [170] or its generalization to multilayer networks by Werbos [166] or Rumelhart et al. [139], have been designed for the task of modeling a functional mapping between input x and output y, given a set of example input–output pairs. From various possible error measures, the mean-squared error (MSE) has been selected because of its differentiability and its widespread use in linear regression and optimal linear mapping.

These learning rules have been adopted for classification in a simple way. It uses the fact that membership in the jth of N classes can be represented by a vector of size N with the kth element equal to unity and all remaining elements zero. The network is then trained for reproducing this representation as closely as possible in the sense of mean-squared error. For novel patterns, the class is determined as the output node with the maximum activation.

Furthermore, there are some historical reasons for using this representation:

1. The classical textbooks on neural networks frequently consider only MSE, not mentioning (or insufficiently emphasizing) the fact that an arbitrary differentiable error function can be used.
2. The MSE-based classifiers have been "sufficiently" successful.

In the following sections, the suitability of MSE as an error measure for classification will be investigated. Based on this investigation (see also Hrycej [81, 82]), a more adequate error measure, together with a corresponding learning rule, are proposed.

6.3.1 Bayesian Classification

In the classical formulation (see, e.g., [27]), the classification task is defined as minimizing the loss L_{ij} that occurs if a pattern from the jth class is classified as a member of the ith class. The loss $L(i,i)$ (the "correct classification loss") is usually defined to be zero. The losses can be organized into a matrix L. The matrix is frequently simplified to all nondiagonal elements equal zero—which amounts to an assumption of *equal misclassification losses*. Given a decision rule with parameters w to be found, classifying the pattern x as a member of class $d(x,w)$, a probability distribution $P(x \mid j)$ of patterns in class j, and prior probability $P(j)$ of each class j, the total expected loss with the decision rule parametrized by w can be written as

$$J(w) = \int \sum L(d(x,w),j)P(x \mid j)P(j). \qquad (6.1)$$

The goal is to find the parameters w^* such that $J(w)$ is minimal.

A common form of the decision rule makes use of a set of functions $f_i(x,w)$ of pattern x and parameter vector w assigned to the individual classes i:

$$d(x,w) = i \text{ such that } f_i(x,w) \text{ is maximal over all } i.$$

This form of decision rule represents a certain scoring of membership of a pattern in the individual classes and deciding in favor of the class with the highest score.

6.3.2 Properties of MSE as an Error Measure

If MSE is applied to a mapping defined by input–output pairs, an optimum with regard to MSE of outputs for given inputs is

$$W = C_{yx}C_{xx}^{-1} \qquad (6.2)$$

with C_{yx} the matrix of correlations between y and x and C_{xx} the autocorrelation matrix of x (see, e.g., Kohonen [91, Chap. 6]), on condition that the dimensionality of input is lower than the number of input–output pairs used to compute the correlation matrices. For the Widrow–Hoff rule [170], convergence of the weight matrix to (6.2) has been shown. If the output vectors y encode the binary coding of classes, this formula (or, equivalently, the Widrow–Hoff rule) can be used to compute the weight matrix of a linear classifier.

The theory of discriminant analysis specifies (for equal misclassification losses) the condition under which such a classifier is an optimal Bayesian classifier. This condition comprises (see, e.g., Hand [59]):

1. Normal distribution of patterns in each class
2. Equal autocorrelation matrices for patterns in all classes

Even if we admit that the first part of this condition may be approximately satisfied in many cases, it is clear that the second part is a very severe limitation. For example, if the handwritten-digit data used in this work had this property, it would mean that the variance of each pixel's gray values and its covariance with all other pixels' gray values would have to be identical for all classes. (If the condition of equal autocorrelation matrices is relaxed, an optimal Bayesian classifier for normally distributed classes is quadratic.)

The second reference from discriminant analysis is confined to two classes. The MSE classifier is then equivalent to the first Fisher's discriminant [36]. Fisher's discriminants make no assumptions about the distribution of patterns, but they are not related directly to the Bayesian classification; they can, rather, be seen as optimal feature extractors for a given classification problem. Another rationale for using MSE for classification is based on the fact that by MSE, a best linear unbiased estimate (BLUE) of Bayesian decision functions is received (see, e.g., Wan [163]).

Although it may seem that there is an (at least linguistic) relationship between "best linear unbiased estimate of Bayesian decision functions" and "best linear Bayesian classifier," and it is certainly tempting to reduce the latter problem to the former, such an implication is not well founded. A simple reason for this is that the misclassification loss, which is the error criterion of Bayesian classification, does not immediately enter the estimation procedure for the Bayesian decision function.

6.3.2.1 Inadequacy of MSE in the General Case. This discrepancy makes the MSE formulation inadequate for finding a minimum

of the total expected loss (6.1). It leads to the following three serious shortcomings:

1. Failing to construct correct separating hypersurfaces
2. Inability to consider an arbitrary loss matrix (L_{ij})
3. Disturbing the convergence of learning by overconstraining the problem

MSE Fails to Construct Correct Separating Hypersurfaces. For each pattern, the MSE criterion tries to approximate a vector of binary variables, each of which attains the value:

- 1 if the pattern is a member of a particular class
- 0 if the pattern is not a member of this class, that is, if it is a member of the complement of this class

So the MSE criterion does not actually look for hypersurfaces separating the classes, but for hypersurfaces separating each class from its complement. For example, given three classes A, B, and C, these are three hypersurfaces separating, respectively:

1. A from its complement $B \cup C$
2. B from $A \cup C$
3. C from $A \cup B$

although the genuine goal is to separate *each class from every other class*. For linear classification [i.e., for linear functions $f_i(x, w)$], the difference can be illustrated by the following examples.

Let us have three classes A, B, and C of patterns described by two features, x_1 and x_2. The regions in the feature space corresponding to the classes are given in Figure 6.3. Three linear functions— $f_A(x_1, x_2) = -\epsilon x_1 + x_2$, $f_B(x_1, x_2) = \epsilon x_1 + x_2$, and $f_C(x_1, x_2) = -x_2$, with ϵ a very small constant—separate classes A, B, and C by hyperplanes symbolized by arrows. (More exactly, the misclassification rate falls to zero if ϵ does.) However, the MSE-based linear classifier fails to find the separating hyperplanes of Figure 6.3. Instead, it finds those of Figure 6.4; its misclassification rate amounts to $5/108 = 4.63\%$.

There is even a two-class example for MSE learning's failure to separate. Let us have two classes, A and B, defined on the Cartesian

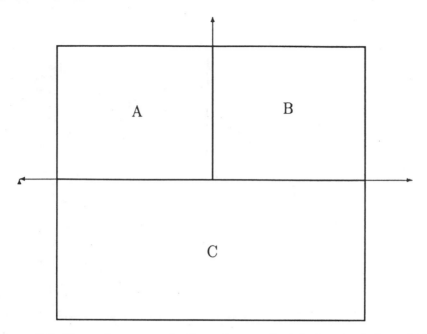

Figure 6.3. *Three-class example: Correct separation of classes A, B, and C. Classes are linearly separable. Vectors represent separating hyperplanes.*

product of all integers $x \in [1,100]$ and $y \in [-2,2]$. The class A is defined by the condition $x + y \leq 50$, class B by $x + y > 50$. Although the classes are obviously linearly separable, a MSE classifier fails to classify correctly two patterns:

1. $x = 49$, $y = 2$: correct classification B, misclassified as A
2. $x = 52$, $y = -2$: correct classification A, misclassified as B

The correct and MSE separating hyperplanes are presented in Figures 6.5 and 6.6, respectively.

A conclusion from both examples is that *the classifier with minimal MSE is different from that with minimal misclassification rate!*. Even worse, this is the case even for linear classifiers and linearly separable classes.

MSE Not Able to Consider an Arbitrary Loss Matrix. Another consequence of separating the class from its complement is that we cannot consider individually specified loss for each misclassification

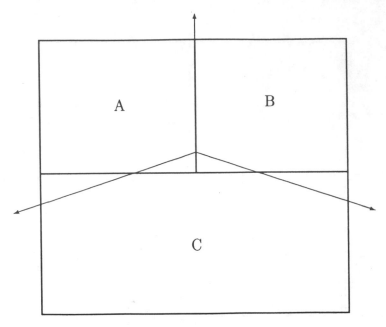

Figure 6.4. *Three-class example: classes A, B, and C. Incorrect separation by MSE-based linear classifier. (Vectors represent MSE separating hyperplanes.)*

Figure 6.5. *Two-class example. Class A, filled circles; class B, points. Correct linear separation.*

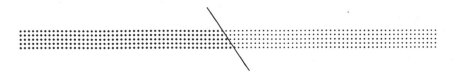

Figure 6.6. *Two-class example. Class A, filled circles; class B, points. Incorrect separation by MSE-based classifier.*

type, that is, the loss for classifying a member of the jth class as a member of the ith class [see the formulation (6.1)]. The reason for this is that the winning class is not identified during learning and thus does not enter the learning rule.

MSE Slows Down the Convergence of Learning. To illustrate this shortcoming of MSE, let us consider the special case of only two classes. In this case a single function $y = f(x,w)$ is sufficient. This function can be thought of as a difference $f_1(x,w) - f_0(x,w)$. The decision rule is then such that a pattern is classified as a member of one class if the function value is below a certain threshold and as a member of the other class otherwise. If we denote the correct classes by 0 and 1, respectively, and assume equal losses for both misclassification types, the loss function $Q(f(x,w),j)$ is

$$Q(y,0) = \begin{cases} 0 & \text{if } y < 0.5, \\ 1 & \text{otherwise,} \end{cases} \quad \text{and}$$

$$Q(y,1) = \begin{cases} 1 & \text{if } y < 0.5, \\ 0 & \text{otherwise.} \end{cases}$$

This error function is presented in Figure 6.7.

It is obvious that the harmful cases are those in which the values of Q are too high for class 0 or too low for class 1. However, the MSE formulation of the two-class case (see Figure 6.8) penalizes even the harmless cases of $Q < 0$ for class 0 and $Q > 1$ for class 1. It can be expected that these unnecessary constraints make the learning substantially slower.

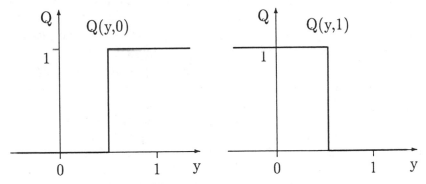

Figure 6.7. *Loss function. Misclassification loss Q for patterns from class 0 (left) and 1 (right). Classifier output, y.*

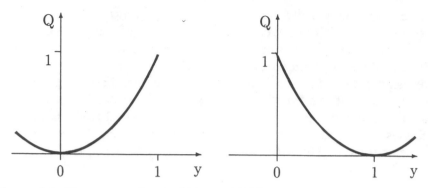

Figure 6.8. *Mean-squared error. Values of MSE error criterion Q for patterns from class 0 (left) and 1 (right).*

6.3.3 Learning Directly by Loss Function Approximations

The arguments presented so far suggest that it would be desirable to adopt the average loss (6.1) as the error criterion. The loss L_{ij} for each pattern is known if its correct classification j is known, i being the class with the maximal value of the scoring function $f_i(x, w)$. The average loss for a given training set can easily be received as an average of losses of all training patterns. However, to apply error backpropagation to finding optimal weights, we must be able to compute the derivative of the error measure (i.e., the loss function) with regard to the functions $f_i(x, w)$. Consequently, the error function must be differentiable, which is not the case for our average loss.

This problem has already been met in research on adaptive linear classifiers for two classes, such as perceptrons (see Rosenblatt [136]). Obviously, some differentiable approximation of the loss function has to be sought. Additionally, no weight change should take place if the classification is correct. In other words, the region corresponding to correct classification (i.e., the zero-loss region) should be preserved. On the other hand, there should be a nonzero gradient in the positive-loss region, in the direction of the zero-loss region.

The simplest form of such approximation is defined by substituting the constant loss by:

1. A loss growing linearly with the difference between the function $f_i(x, w)$ corresponding to false class i and the function

$f_j(x,w)$ corresponding to the correct class j, for i different from j

2. Zero loss otherwise

This can be expressed as

$$Q(y,j) = L_{ij} pos(y_i - y_j) \qquad (6.3)$$

with y the vector of output unit activations, i the index of the largest y_j, and the function $pos(u)$ defined as $pos(u) = u$ for $u > 0$ and $pos(u) = 0$ otherwise. This leads to a loss function (Hrycej [81, 82]) whose derivative with regard to y_j can be written

$$\frac{dQ}{dy_i} = L_{ij} sgnpos(y_i - y_j),$$

$$\frac{dQ}{dy_j} = -L_{ij} sgnpos(y_i - y_j), \qquad (6.4)$$

$$\frac{dQ}{dy_k} = 0 \qquad (k \neq i,j),$$

with $sgnpos(u) = 1$ if $u > 0$ and $sgnpos(u) - 0$ otherwise.

A two-class version of this rule is the well-known perceptron rule (see Figure 6.9). This error function can be expected to overcome the three shortcomings of MSE:

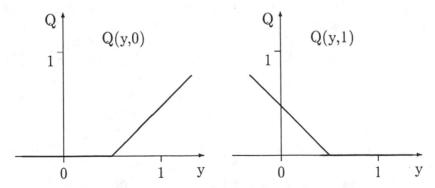

Figure 6.9. *Differentiable approximation of the loss function. Misclassification loss approximation Q for patterns from class 0 (left) and 1 (right).*

1. $Q(y,j)$ is minimal (i.e., zero) for minimal misclassification loss if the classes are separable by the given classifier.
2. The complete loss matrix $|L_{ij}|$ is accounted for [see (6.3)].
3. The requirement of preserving the zero-loss region implies that no redundant constraints are imposed.

Knowing the gradient of the loss function (6.4), it is easy to derive the learning rule for the weight w_{li} for the lth class and ith input:

$$\frac{dQ}{dw_{li}} = \frac{dQ}{dy_l}\frac{dy_l}{dw_{li}}$$

$$= \frac{dQ}{dy_l}x_i \tag{6.5}$$

6.3.3.1 Why Linear Separation of Multiple Classes Is Important.
It has already been mentioned that for two classes, the loss function–based learning rule can be transformed to the well-known perceptron rule of Rosenblatt [136]. This transformation consists of merging both scoring functions into one by subtracting one of them from the other. From this viewpoint, the whole merit of the loss function–based learning rule may seem to be a "mere" generalization to multiple classes.

However, it is exactly the case of two classes that leads to the idea that linear, single-layer perceptrons are of very limited applicability (Minsky and Papert [110]). This also becomes intuitively clear if we observe the two linearly separable classes A and B of Figure 6.10a. The principal limitation of separating hypersurfaces to hyperplanes remains, of course, valid for multiple classes, too. However, since there are up to $N(N-1)/2$ such separating hyperplanes for N classes, multiple-class linearly separable problems are substantially less trivial (see Figure 6.10b). In a sense, the expressiveness of linear classifiers for real-world problems grows with the number of classes.

In particular, *an arbitrary convex class can be separated if it is "contrasted" with a sufficient number of classes disjoint with it.* For example, class F of Figure 6.10b is contrasted by its neighbor classes A, B, C, E, and G. It is intuitively clear that the probability that such a set of contrast classes is available grows with the total number of classes.

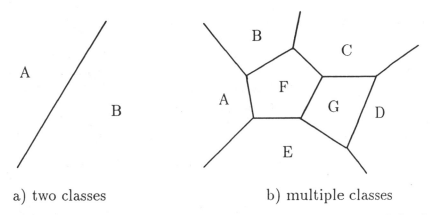

a) two classes   b) multiple classes

Figure 6.10. *Linear separability. The concept of linear separability is obviously more powerful for multiple classes.*

There is a close relationship to the fact that a network with a single hidden layer is able to separate an arbitrary convex class (Lippmann [102]). Each hidden unit represents a hyperplane separating the convex class from a part of its set complement. All hidden units together represent complete separation of the convex class from its nonconvex complement. This can be viewed as assigning a hidden contrast class to each hidden unit. Once more, with a growing total number of explicit classes, the probability that the contrast classes can be found between them, and thus do not have to be constructed in the hidden layer, is growing. In other words, *the superiority of a multilayer perceptron over a linear, single-layer linear perceptron with the loss function–based learning rule diminishes with a growing number of classes.*

6.3.3.2 Properties of the Loss Function-Based Learning Rule.
Let us now investigate the properties of the loss function–based learning rule developed in the preceding section. In particular, we are interested in the state to which the learning rule converges and whether this convergence is guaranteed.

First, an important remark concerning general convergence of learning rules must be made. If any learning rule is applied in the classical way [i.e., sampling patterns from some probability distribution and changing the classifier parameters (weights and thresholds) after each sample], the only way to guarantee convergence is by *stochastic approximation.* The theory of stochastic approximation has been developed successively by Robbins and Monro [134], Kiefer and Wolfowitz [89], and Dvoretzky [28]. It is applicable to all incremental gradient learning rules. The usual form of these learning rules contains a constant learning rate. The classifier parameters are changed in the direction of the steepest gradient by an amount proportional to (1) the learning rate and (2) the magnitude of the gradient. It is obvious that a stable parameter state can be attained only if one or both converges to zero. If the gradient is computed for the pattern one by one, it is clear that it can scarcely be guaranteed that it is zero for each, even if the desired state of zero gradient of the mean value over all patterns has been reached. Thus it is necessary to make the learning rate converge to zero, which is exactly what the theory of stochastic approximation proposes. According to this theory, the convergence of the gradient method for stochastic patterns is guaranteed if the sequence of the learning rates α_t for individual learning iterations t satisfies the following conditions:

$$\sum_{t=1}^{\infty} \alpha_t^2 < \infty$$

(to guarantee the decrease of α_t to zero) and

$$\sum_{t=1}^{\infty} \alpha_t = \infty$$

(to guarantee that the optimum is reached even if it is arbitrarily remote from the initial state of parameters). An example of such a sequence is

$$\alpha_t = \frac{1}{t}.$$

However, besides these two conditions, which can be satisfied by infinitely many learning rate sequences, little is known about the optimal form of this sequence. For separable classes, optimal sequences have been found (e.g., by Kacmarz [85]), which, however, do not satisfy the conditions of stochastic approximation. The optimal sequence is probably heavily dependent on the individual task. These problems frequently lead to using simply a constant learning rate, with the consequence that parameters are never completely stable.

Let us recall that so far, we have been discussing the case of one-by-one presentation of random samples. In practical classification tasks, we are not confined to random samples. Rather, we are given a complete set of training patterns and are free to determine the way in which they will be presented to the learning algorithm. One such possible way is to *cumulate* the gradients for all patterns and to perform the change of classifier parameters with such a cumulated gradient. (This method is also known as that of *learning epochs*.) An important theoretical advantage of this method is that we are now able to reach a stable state with a constant learning rate. The reason for this is that the cumulative gradient, which is a mean gradient over the training set, itself converges to zero for the optimal (at least locally) parameter values. We have, in fact, made the problem deterministic by observing the gradient of mean value instead of the stochastic gradient of individual patterns. This is why *cumulative gradients have been used in all algorithms throughout this work.*

Let us now proceed to an investigation of the properties of the loss function–based learning rule with cumulative gradient. A question of eminent importance is if there is a state to which the classifier parameters converge in a guaranteed manner. This is easy to show with the help of the following theorem (Hrycej [82]).

Theorem 6.3.1 The cumulative loss function is convex with regard to classifier parameters.

Proof. The cumulative loss function can be written as a sum of losses (6.3) of individual patterns

$$QC = \sum_k L(i_k, j_k)pos(y_{i_k} - y_{j_k}) \qquad (6.6)$$

summing over all patterns k, with i_k the class with the highest value of classification score f_i for the kth pattern and j_k the correct class of the kth pattern.

To prove that QC is convex, it is sufficient to prove that all its summands are convex. Let us consider the classifier parameter u_{lr}, which is the rth parameter of the scoring function f_l. There are two different cases to be analyzed:

1. $l = j_k$; that is, the correct class of the kth pattern is l. Since the function f_l is linear in parameters, it can be written as

$$f_l = x_r u_{lr} + c \qquad (6.7)$$

with x_r the rth element of the kth input pattern and c the absolute term. Let us denote the index of the class with the maximum score for the kth pattern from all classes different from l by l_0. For $x_r > 0$, the kth loss function summand is

$$f_{l_0} - x_r u_{lr} - c \qquad \text{for} \quad u_{lr} < \frac{f_{l_0} - c}{x_r}$$

$$0 \qquad \qquad \text{otherwise.}$$

For $x_r < 0$, it is

$$f_{l_0} - x_r u_{lr} - c \qquad \text{for} \quad u_{lr} > \frac{f_{l_0} - c}{x_r}$$

$$0 \qquad \qquad \text{otherwise.}$$

For $x_r = 0$, the loss function summand is constant for any u_{lr}. In all three cases, the loss function summand is convex with regard to classifier parameter u_{lr}.

2. $l \neq j_k$; that is, the correct class of the kth pattern is different from l. With f_l written as (6.7), the kth loss function summand is

$$x_r u_{lr} + c - f_{j_k} \qquad \text{for} \quad u_{lr} > \frac{f_{j_k} - c}{x_r}$$

$$0 \qquad \qquad \text{otherwise}$$

for $x_r > 0$, and

$$x_r u_{lr} + c - f_{j_k} \qquad \text{for} \quad u_{lr} < \frac{f_{j_k} - c}{x_r}$$

$$0 \qquad \qquad \text{otherwise}$$

for $x_r > 0$. For $x_r = 0$, the summand is constant. Once more, in all cases the kth summand of the cumulative loss function (6.6) is convex with regard to u_{lr}.

Since the summands of (6.6) are convex with regard to all classifier parameters, so is the entire cumulative loss function.   □

The most important immediate consequence of this theorem is that the global minimum of this function can be found by the gradient method.

Theorem 6.3.2   The global minimum of the cumulative loss function (6.6) can be found by gradient descent.

Proof. An immediate consequence of Theorem 6.3.1, since for convex functions the minimum can always be found by gradient descent.   □

An important case is the case of linearly separable classes.

Theorem 6.3.3   If the classes of a classification problem are linearly separable, the cumulative loss function–based learning rule (6.5) will find the scoring functions f_l that separate the classes.

Proof. The learning rule based on the cumulative loss function is a gradient descent for the function (6.6). For linearly separable classes, the minimum of the cumulative loss function is zero, which corresponds to the case of no misclassification loss. According to Theorem 6.3.2, this minimum (i.e., the correct separating functions f_l) is guaranteed to be found by gradient descent.   □

Let us now turn to the question of convergence of the loss function–based learning rule for linearly nonseparable classification problems. The mathematical answer is given by Theorem 6.3.2—the rule converges to the minimum of the cumulative loss function (6.6). For each combination of the computed classification i_k and the correct classification j_k, the sum of positive differences $y_{i_k} - y_{j_k}$ can be written as

$$\sum_k (y_{i_k} - y_{j_k}) = n(i,j)\frac{1}{n(i,j)}\sum_k (y_{i_k} - y_{j_k}) = n(i,j)E[y_{i_k} - y_{j_k}]$$

(6.8)

summing only over patterns with computed classification i_k and correct classification j_k, with $n(i,j)$ being the count of misclassifications of the given type, and $E[y_{i_k} - y_{j_k}]$ the average difference between the score of the computed class and the score of the correct class for misclassified patterns. For the exact loss function, the corresponding term is

$$n(i,j). \tag{6.9}$$

So we can interpret the cumulative loss function approximation (6.6) as a loss function with losses weighted by the distance of scores.

We can make various assumptions about the density of misclassified patterns in the pattern space and consequent estimates of the quality of approximation of the exact loss function. An extreme assumption is that of constant density. We assume that the differences in scorings of misclassified patterns are uniformly distributed; that is, high difference values are as probable as low values. Under this extreme (unrealistic) assumption, the average score difference of (6.9) is

$$E[y_{i_k} - y_{j_k}] = \frac{n(i,j)}{d_{ij}} \tag{6.10}$$

with d_{ij} a density coefficient. Then (6.8) can be written as

$$n(i,j)^2 d_{ij}. \tag{6.11}$$

If the density decreases with the score difference, the power of $n(i,j)$ is less than 2.

The power of $n(i,j)$ could be reduced by taking a loss function approximation analogous to (6.3) but with a power of the difference lower than 1; for example,

$$LC = \sum_k L(i_k, j_k)\sqrt{y_{i_k} - y_{j_k}}. \tag{6.12}$$

The cost of this would be that the cumulative loss function is no longer convex and that convergence to the global minimum is not guaranteed. This has also been confirmed by computational experiments: Convergence with the loss function (6.12) has deteriorated substantially. A discussion of various error functions that is slightly different from but related to the present viewpoint has been given by Shynk [148].

6.3.4 Improvements to the Algorithm

Two improvements on the loss function–based learning rule have been implemented in this work. The goal of the first is an improvement of generalization. The other is concerned with ensuring the stationary state of classifier parameters.

6.3.4.1 *Insensitivity Zone.* In the basic version of the learning rule, the gradient of the loss approximation is positive only if a misclassification has taken place, and is zero even if the difference between the highest score of the correct class and the next highest score is zero, or very small. This were certainly correct if we intended to classify only the training set. However, the ultimate goal is to classify novel patterns correctly, too. Even if the novel patterns are also linearly separable, it is possible that the correct separating hyperplanes have not been identified exactly by the loss function–based learning rule because of incomplete coverage of the classes by the training set.

This is why it makes sense not only to separate the training set, but to separate it with an allowance, finding a certain zone between each pair of classes free from any training patterns, and leading the separating hyperplane through the center of this zone. This zone has been called the "insensitivity zone." To reach this, the learning rule is modified to learn even if a pattern is nearly misclassified:

$$QC = \sum_k L(i_k, j_k) pos(y_{i_k} + \delta - y_{j_k}) \qquad (6.13)$$

with δ the width of the insensitivity zone, usually set to a small number like 0.1.

6.3.4.2 *Constraining the Length of the Weight Vectors.* A problem with the loss function–based learning rule is that for linearly nonseparable classes, it may fail to reach any stationary state. In simple terms, the weights may grow without limits if the learning goes on. This growth is not very harmful, since after a certain moment it consists of a permanent rescaling of the weights without changing their proportion, so that the directions of the weights vectors are stable. However:

1. It is difficult to identify the state in which the weights do not change any more, that is, to formulate a stop rule.

2. The relative importance of the insensitivity zone decreases with growing absolute values of the scorings.

For these reasons, it appears necessary to stop the growth in some way. The most straightforward way, keeping the sum of the absolute values of all parameters constant, is inappropriate since it makes the loss function generally nonconvex.

A smoother method is to add a term penalizing overly high values of classifier parameters. The simplest way is to add a quadratic term to the cumulative loss function (6.6)

$$-\gamma \sum_{l,r} w_{lr}^2 \qquad (6.14)$$

summing over all weights w_{lr}. The gradient of this term with regard to w_{lr} is

$$-\frac{\gamma}{2} w_{lr}. \qquad (6.15)$$

6.3.5 Generalization to Multiple Layers

The loss function–based learning rule can be generalized to multilayer networks in a straightforward way. The basic formula of error backpropagation (using the denotation of Rumelhart et al. [139]) is

$$\frac{dE}{dw_{ij}} = \frac{dE}{do_j}\frac{do_j}{dnet_j}\frac{dnet_j}{dw_{ji}} = \frac{dE}{do_j}f'(net_j)o_i \qquad \text{for the output layer}$$

$$= \sum_k \frac{dE}{do_k}\frac{do_k}{dnet_j}w_{kj}f'(net_j)o_i \qquad \text{for hidden layers}$$

with indices i and j denoting the nodes of previous and present layers, respectively (different from previous use as class indices).

The only modification necessary is to replace $dE/do_j = (t_j - o_j)$ for the output layer by the dQ/dy_j of (6.4). [In this notation, the activation of the jth output unit o_j corresponds to the variable y_j of

(6.4).] The weights are changed in the direction opposite to that of the derivative:

$$-\frac{dE}{dw_{ji}}.$$

6.3.6 Computational Experience with Loss Functions

To test the hypothesis that backpropagation using the misclassification loss should perform better for classification tasks than the MSE-based backpropagation, a series of computational experiments has been run. Both linear classifiers (i.e., networks without hidden layers) and nonlinear classifiers (networks with one hidden layer) using the gradient method as a learning rule have been tested.

First, a linear loss function–based classifier has been applied to the problem of Figure 6.3. As expected, the classifier consistently converged to the correct separation according to Figure 6.3. By contrast, the linear MSE classifier exhibited an error of 4.63%, as predicted.

Further experiments concerned the thyroid data set. For each classifier, five trials with various randomly generated initial weights have been performed. Average misclassification rates from these five trials are given in Tables 6.1 and 6.2. It is obvious that the results for both linear and nonlinear loss function–based classifiers are clearly superior to the corresponding MSE results. After 2000 iterations, the nonlinear misclassification-loss classifier approaches the misclassification rate of 1.46% reached by Weiss and Kapouleas for MSE backpropagation after 70,000 iterations!

TABLE 6.1 Thyroid Data: Misclassification Rates (Percent)[a]

Error Function	Number of Iterations			
	100	300	1000	2000
Training set				
MSE	6.76	(noniterative algorithm)		
Misclassification loss	3.20	2.17	2.17	2.17
Test set				
MSE	6.59	(noniterative algorithm)		
Misclassification loss	4.69	3.47	3.44	3.44

[a]Linear MSE and misclassification loss classifiers.

TABLE 6.2   Thyroid Data: Misclassification Rates (Percent)[a]

Error Function	Number of Iterations			
	100	300	1000	2000
Training set				
MSE	5.35	3.95	2.46	1.85
Misclassification loss	4.00	1.11	1.03	0.84
Test set				
MSE	5.80	4.49	3.17	2.77
Misclassification loss	4.78	1.98	1.86	1.77

[a]Nonlinear MSE and misclassification loss classifiers.

6.4   COMPUTATIONAL RESULTS WITH QUANTIZATION

The analysis of Section 6.3 suggests that if a linear classifier is applied to a *quantized* input, its power is increased substantially. How far this increased power is relevant in real-world applications can only be decided experimentally.

6.4.1   Thyroid Data

A series of computational experiments on the thyroid data set comparing the performance of two neural network classifiers have been performed:

1. A backpropagation network with one hidden layer
2. A network consisting of a quantization layer and a classical perceptron layer (see Figure 6.11)

For the second model, three types of quantization have been used:

1. A Kohonen topological map [91] transforming the 21-dimensional input into a vector of size 100.
2. Quantization of each of the 21 inputs into q intervals of equal width.
3. Quantization of each input into q intervals, with interval centers found by the competitive learning. [This model is further referred to as a quantization + perceptron $(Q + P)$ rule.]

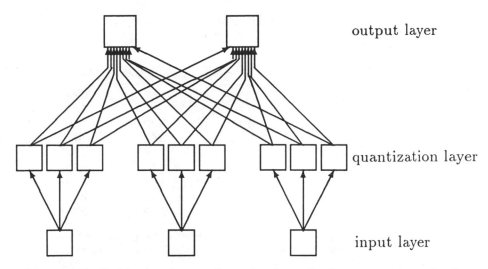

output layer

quantization layer

input layer

Figure 6.11. *Architecture for one-dimensional* quantization + perceptron *classifier. Each input is mapped on a set of quantization units. Quantization units are completely interconnected with output units.*

The misclassification rates for model $2a$ (despite running thousands of iterations for self-organization, while model $2c$ converged reliably after 50 iterations) and model $2b$ have been higher than 4%. This is a relatively disappointing result compared with models 1 and $2c$. This shows that the Kohonen map was too sparse to profit from its relationship to a full 21-dimensional grid, but the simple one-dimensional self-organizing maps optimized the quantization considerably; on the other hand, a trivial quantization after $2b$ alone is not very helpful.

The results for backpropagation networks with h hidden units (BP $-h$) and $Q + P$ classifiers with quantization factor q ($Q + P - q$) are given in Tables 6.3 to 6.9. Tables 6.3 and 6.4 present averages of misclassification rates from five trials for training and test sets after 100 and 1000 iterations as well as the best results reached. The results after 1000 iterations are comparable to those published by Weiss and Kapouleas after 2000 iterations. Table 6.5 shows relative standard deviations of test set misclassification rates after 100 and 1000 iterations from the five trials.

Tables 6.6 and 6.7 show the CPU time in seconds on a Cadmus RISC workstation (processor R2000) necessary to reach a certain

TABLE 6.3   Thyroid Data: Misclassification Rates (Percent)[a]

Classifier	100 Iterations	1000 Iterations	Best Result	After Iteration Number:
$Q + P - 2$	2.51	1.08	0.82	5000
$Q + P - 5$	1.27	0.71	0.53	2000
$Q + P - 7$	0.87	0.42	0.42	1000
$Q + P - 10$	0.26	0.02	0.02	1000
$BP - 2$	5.51	2.54	1.56	6000
$BP - 3$	5.03	1.08	0.87	4000
$BP - 6$	4.18	1.37	1.14	2000
$BP - 9$	3.65	1.16	0.90	2000
$BP - 12$	3.26	0.95	0.79	2000

[a] $BP - h$, backpropagation networks with h hidden units, $Q + P - q$, quantization–perceptron classifiers with quantization factor q. Results for training set.

TABLE 6.4   Thyroid Data: Misclassification Rates (Percent)[a]

Classifier	100 Iterations	1000 Iterations	Best Result	After Iteration Number:
$Q + P - 2$	2.71	1.60	1.57	5000
$Q + P - 5$	1.51	1.40	1.45	2000
$Q + P - 7$	1.40	1.34	1.34	1000
$Q + P - 10$	0.99	0.84	0.84	1000
$BP - 2$	5.89	3.26	2.53	6000
$BP - 3$	5.57	2.10	1.98	4000
$BP - 6$	4.72	2.33	2.30	2000
$BP - 9$	4.31	2.21	2.07	2000
$BP - 12$	4.08	2.15	2.00	2000

[a] Results for test set.

misclassification rate. The ratios between the worst and the best of the CPU times for various numbers of quantization units for $Q + P$ classifiers, and for various numbers of hidden units for BP classifiers, are computed from Tables 6.6 and 6.7 and presented in Table 6.8.

Further, to assess the generalization capabilities of both models, some relationships between misclassification rates for training and

TABLE 6.5 Thyroid Data: Standard Deviations of Misclassification Rates

Classifier	100 Iterations	1000 Iterations
$Q + P - 2$	8.4	1.3
$Q + P - 5$	3.9	2.5
$Q + P - 7$	3.1	3.1
$Q + P - 10$	1.8	2.4
$BP - 2$	7.4	26.8
$BP - 3$	5.5	41.5
$BP - 6$	9.9	7.8
$BP - 9$	14.6	13.1
$BP - 12$	11.1	8.2

TABLE 6.6 Thyroid Data: CPU Times[a]

Classifier	3%	2%	1.5%	1%	0.5%	0.1%
$Q + P - 2$	76	221	409	—	—	—
$Q + P - 5$	97	146	211	678	5784	—
$Q + P - 7$	96	167	215	340	1745	—
$Q + P - 10$	167	198	220	250	343	3361
$BP - 2$	843	2554	—	—	—	—
$BP - 3$	412	772	1240	2777	—	—
$BP - 6$	698	1393	3045	—	—	—
$BP - 9$	928	2095	3796	8472	—	—
$BP - 12$	950	2332	4154	6840	—	—

[a]CPU times (seconds) necessary to reach a certain misclassification rate. Results for training set.

test set are shown in Table 6.9. We can observe the following:

1. $Q + P$ classifiers reach lower misclassification rates than BP both (a) absolutely and (b) for a given iteration number. After as many iterations as 70,000 (Weiss and Kapouleas [165]), is outperformed by $QP - 7$ and $QP - 10$ after 100 iterations (see Tables 6.3 and 6.4)!

2. For a given precision, $Q + P$ classifiers converge faster both in iterations (Tables 6.3 and 6.4) and in CPU time (Tables 6.6 and 6.7). The CPU times for a given test set misclassification rate are about 20 times shorter.

TABLE 6.7 Thyroid Data: CPU Times[a]

Classifier	3%	2%	1.5%	1%
$Q + P - 2$	101	351	—	—
$Q + P - 5$	111	157	435	—
$Q + P - 7$	133	201	347	—
$Q + P - 10$	193	233	264	506
$BP - 2$	2119	—	—	—
$BP - 3$	633	6418	—	—
$BP - 6$	1080	—	—	—
$BP - 9$	2435	13689	—	—
$BP - 12$	2116	14400	—	—

[a]CPU times (seconds) necessary to reach a certain misclassification rate. Results for test set.

TABLE 6.8 Thyroid Data: Worst/Best Ratios of Misclassification Rates[a]

Classifier	Training Set			Test Set	
	3%	2%	1.5%	3%	2%
$Q + P$	2.20	1.51	1.94	1.91	2.24
BP	2.31	3.31	7.83	3.85	—

[a]Ratios of the worst to the best case from trials with various numbers or hidden or quantization units.

TABLE 6.9 Thyroid Data: Generalization Coefficients[a]

Classifier	A	B	C
$Q + P - 2$	1.59	1.92	—
$Q + P - 5$	1.80	1.72	1.46
$Q + P - 7$	1.63	1.86	1.50
$Q + P - 10$	1.27	2.32	1.69
$BP - 2$	—	—	—
$BP - 3$	0.84	2.49	2.08
$BP - 6$	—	2.46	—
$BP - 9$	—	2.61	2.13
$BP - 12$	0.79	2.61	2.20

[a]A, training set performance necessary to reach 2% test set performance; B, test set performance in % if training set performance is 1.5%; C, test set performance in % if training set performance is 1%.

3. The generalization capability, due to smoothness of linear classifiers used, is substantially better than for BP. The ratios between training and test set performances (Table 6.9) are consistently better than those of BP—the test set misclassification rates follow the training set rates much more closely.

4. Both $Q + P$ and BP exhibit increasing performance with increasing size of hidden layer. However, the computational CPU expense of BP shows stronger random perturbations for various hidden unit numbers (see the worst/best ratios of Table 6.8).

5. The convergence stability of $Q + P$ classifiers is superior to that of BP classifiers—the influence of random initial connection weights is substantially lower (see the last two columns of Table 6.5).

6. For BP, more hidden units consistently enhance the performance on the training set, but the test set performance may casually deteriorate. This is not the case for $Q + P$ (Tables 6.3 to 6.7).

6.4.2 Handwritten Digits

The relationship between the width of the handwritten-digit pattern vectors (256 pixel values) and the training set size (1000 training patterns for the reduced set and 10,000 for the full set) is not as advantageous as in the case of thyroid data. This is particularly harmful for any dimensionality-extending classification approach, an instance of which is just the quantization of this chapter. This is the case for the following reason. If the dimensionality of patterns exceeds the training set size, all training patterns can be learned exactly even by a linear classifier (see, e.g., Kohonen [91]). The cost for this is that no genuine generalization takes place. More exactly, this is the case in which optimal mapping is underconstrained and thus ambiguous. The optimal solution to this is by underconstrained pseudoinverse of the input correlation matrix, which represents a solution corresponding to the orthogonal projection of novel patterns on the training patterns. This is, at best, a generalization in the nearest-neighbor sense. This is all also true if the original dimensionality has been lower than the training set size—what counts is the dimensionality of transformed patterns since it is these patterns that become the input of the linear classifier. Even if the dimensionality of input is

TABLE 6.10 Handwritten Digits: Misclassification Rates (Percent)[a]

	Noncompressed	20 Features	40 Features
Training set	0.00	3.77	0.80
Test set	7.53	6.18	5.83

[a]Results of $Q + P$ classifiers for training and test sets.

not higher than, but approaches, the training set size, the classifier cannot be expected to generalize reasonably.

For these reasons, the reduced handwritten-digit training set cannot be used at all—even with a quantization factor as small as 4, the pattern width of $256 \times 4 = 1024$ would exceed the training set size 1000. Even for the full training set, only low quantization factors such as 5 can be used, and the expectations for generalization are not very high.

The results for both training and test sets of handwritten digits are given in Table 6.10. The results for $Q + P$ classification of compressed data are presented, too. Comparing these results with those of Chapter 5, the following conclusions can be made:

1. The training set performance is always superior to that of linear classifiers applied to the original input. This is a consequence of the extension of the class of linearly separable problems with the help of quantization as analyzed in Section 6.2.

2. The test set performance is worse than that of linear classifiers. The explanation for this can be sought in the following facts:

   (a) For the original data, this is probable to have resulted from the insufficient dimensionality/training set size ratio.

   (b) Furthermore, the fact that the distribution of gray values for individual pixels is probably nearly uniform must be taken into account. Under this circumstance, it is clear that competitive quantization (whose goal is to optimize the distribution of quantization intervals) is almost equivalent to equidistant intervals. So the contribution of quantization to optimal classification can be expected to be rather low.

3. Compared with the performance of backpropagation classifiers, quantization by factor 5 seems to be equivalent to hidden layer size 5 to 10.

6.5 QUANTIZATION NETWORK AS A LEARNING MODULE

Unlike the feature-discovery module of Chapter 5, there is a less specific relationship between the number of feature (i.e., cluster) units and the success expectations for the subsequent supervised learning module. The number of units per input variable should express our knowledge of how many "fundamentally different" values an input variable can acquire. On the other side, the computational experiments have indicated that taking more units does not lead to a deterioration of the generalization capabilities of the subsequent supervised learning, so the generalization behavior is monotonic.

So the assessment of success of preprocessing by quantization consists essentially in observing the proper convergence. The first criterion of accomplished convergence is common to all learning algorithms: It is the stability of results (e.g., the size of individual clusters), that is, the numbers of patterns from the training set that belong to the region in which individual units win the competition. Another criterion concerns the question of whether all feature units have been active. Units that have never won the competition have also never learned. Inactive units can easily be identified as those with zero clusters. If there are some inactive units, the learning algorithm can be slightly modified in the following way proposed by Rumelhart and Zipser [141]: Learning is also extended to nonwinning units, but with a substantially lower learning rate. This makes the weight vectors of all units be weakly attracted to the centroid of the entire training set, in addition to being strongly attracted to the centroids of the corresponding clusters.

CHAPTER 7 —————————————————

Finding Optimal Features for a Given Task

Chapters 5 and 6 have been concerned with the problem of finding features or other transformations of the input that would facilitate supervised learning of associations between such transformed input and the desired output. An important property of these transformations has been their independence from any particular supervised learning task.

It is a logical expectation that if features independent from a particular task can substantially improve the learning efficiency, this must be even more the case if features with a bias in favor of a particular task are searched for. Supporting supervised learning by such biased features is the topic of this chapter.

7.1 FEATURES FOUND BY THE HIDDEN LAYER OF A MULTILAYER PERCEPTRON

A widespread interpretation of a multilayer network with a hidden layer assigns hidden units conceptually to features building an intermediate representation advantageous for solving a particular supervised learning task. This view is obviously closely related to the idea of looking for optimal features for a given task. Let us briefly investigate what this representation may be for a perceptron with a single layer of *linear* hidden units and a single output unit. This network will be applied to the classification task with two classes. We can then assume that the representation by nonlinear hidden units is some type of nonlinear extension of this idea.

Since for linear hidden units, any rescaling of the connection weights between the hidden layer and the output unit can be traded off by a corresponding rescaling of the connection weights between the input layer and the hidden layer, we can assume, without loss of generality, that all output layer weights are equal to 1. Let us denote input patterns from class 0 as x_{0k}, those from class 1 as x_{1l}, the hidden layer vectors corresponding to these pattern as y_{0k} and y_{1l}, respectively, and the activations of the output unit as z_{0k} and z_{1l}, respectively. The error measure is the mean-squared error (MSE) of the output activation with regard to correct activations 0 and 1 for classes 0 and 1, respectively.

$$
\begin{aligned}
\text{MSE} &= \sum_k (z_{0k} - 0)^2 + \sum_l (z_{1l} - 1)^2 \\
&= \sum_k (z_{0k} - \bar{z}_0 + \bar{z}_0 - 0)^2 + \sum_l (z_{1l} - \bar{z}_1 + \bar{z}_1 - 1)^2 \\
&= \sum_k (z_{0k} - \bar{z}_0)^2 + (\bar{z}_0 - 0)\sum_k (z_{0k} - \bar{z}_0) + n_0(\bar{z}_0 - 0)^2 \\
&\quad + \sum_l (z_{1l} - \bar{z}_1)^2 + (\bar{z}_1 - 1)\sum_l (z_{1l} - \bar{z}_1) + n_1(\bar{z}_1 - 1)^2 \\
&= \sum_k (z_{0k} - \bar{z}_0)^2 + \sum_l (z_{1l} - \bar{z}_1)^2 \\
&\quad + n_0(\bar{z}_0 - 0)^2 + n_1(\bar{z}_1 - 1)^2 \\
&= nV_i + n_0(\bar{z}_0 - 0)^2 + n_1(\bar{z}_1 - 1)^2
\end{aligned}
\tag{7.1}
$$

with $\bar{z}_{0,1}$ averages of z over all patterns from classes 0 or 1, respectively, and V_i the intraclass variance of z. Minimizing MSE, it can be expected that the differences $\bar{z}_0 - 0$ and $\bar{z}_1 - 1$ become very small.

This is a justification for assuming that

$$\bar{z}_0 \doteq 0 \quad \text{and} \quad \bar{z}_1 \doteq 1. \tag{7.2}$$

This assumption implies that

$$\begin{aligned} nV_e &= n_0(\bar{z}_0 - \bar{z})^2 + n_1(\bar{z}_1 - \bar{z})^2 \\ &\doteq n_0(0 - \bar{z})^2 + n_1(1 - \bar{z})^2 \\ &= \text{const.} \end{aligned} \tag{7.3}$$

with $\bar{z}$ the average of z over both classes and V_e the interclass variance.

So, using this simplifying assumption, we can argue that the hidden units represent linear combinations of input such that their intraclass variance V_i is minimized by (7.1), keeping the interclass variance V_e constant by appropriate scaling of the weights.

This suggests a close relationship to the classical discriminant analysis of Fisher [36] with canonical variables. In the discriminant analysis, linear combinations of input are sought, which maximize the ratio V_e/V_i. This objective is obviously equivalent to the objective of minimizing V_i while keeping V_e constant by rescaling.

7.2 SUPERVISED FEATURE DISCOVERY

The feature-discovery principles of Chapter 3 can be modified in a straightforward way to supervised feature discovery (Hrycej [76, 77]). As stated in Theorem 5.5.1, the optimal weight matrix **W** is a product of the principal component matrix U, which is completely determined by the statistical properties of input patterns and the orthonormal rotation matrix T (see Figure 7.1). This rotation can be viewed as a set of free parameters to a given classification or problem. In other words, we can look for a feature rotation optimal for the given problem. This can be done simply by combining the unsupervised learning rule (5.5) with the usual backpropagation learning:

$$\frac{d\mathbf{W}}{dt} = a\mathbf{y}(\mathbf{x}^{\mathrm{T}} - \mathbf{y}^{\mathrm{T}}\mathbf{W}) - b\frac{dE_y}{d\mathbf{W}}. \tag{7.4}$$

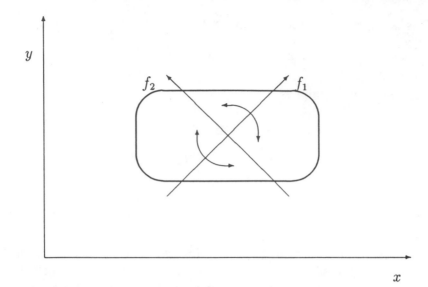

Figure 7.1. *Rotation of features by supervised feature discovery. The oval represents the region covered by data patterns. The goal is to find a rotational shift optimal for a given task.*

with E_y the mean-squared error of output and b the backpropagation learning rate. Since the learning rule (5.5) can be viewed as a gradient-descent method for finding an autoassociative mapping optimal for the reconstruction of input (see [75]), we can also write (7.4) as

$$\frac{d\mathbf{W}}{dt} = -a\frac{dE_x}{d\mathbf{W}} - b\frac{dE_y}{d\mathbf{W}}$$

with E_x the mean-squared error of input if the feature layer representation is used for input reconstruction.

If the feature vector $\mathbf{y}$ is passed through a sigmoid function before entering the supervised learning module, the network is capable of nonlinear mappings without an additional hidden layer. This means that the feature layer plays the role of the hidden layer simultaneously. Consequently, a three-layer architecture is sufficient (see the architecture of Figure 7.2). However, this causes a certain problem. The unsupervised learning part of the rule (7.4) forces the weight vectors of individual feature nodes to orthonormality. This would obviously constrain the nonlinear mapping capability of the

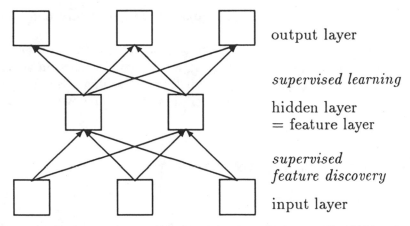

output layer

supervised learning

hidden layer
= feature layer

*supervised
feature discovery*

input layer

Figure 7.2. *Architecture for supervised feature discovery. The hidden layer plays the role of feature layer simultaneously.*

model in comparison with the usual backpropagation for which the norm of weight vectors is arbitrary, and allows, in an indirect way, a variable degree of discreteness: For large vector norms, the sigmoid function approaches the step function, while for small vector norms, it approaches the linear function. To retain the model generality, a variable scaling factor for each feature unit must be introduced. This scaling factor can be written as a "temperature":

$$f(x) = \frac{1}{1 + e^{-x/T}} \tag{7.5}$$

This parameter can be changed by gradient descent in an exact analogy to other model parameters, such as weights or thresholds. For the jth feature unit, the rule is

$$\frac{dT_i}{dt} = -c \frac{dE_u}{dT_j}$$

$$= -c \frac{dE_y}{do_j} \frac{do_j}{dT_j}$$

$$= c \frac{dE_y}{do_j} o_j (1 - o_j) \frac{net_j}{T_j^2} \tag{7.6}$$

with net_j, o_j the input and the output of the jth feature unit and c the learning rate.

With this model we have only $2m - 1$ degrees of freedom ($m - 1$ rotation angles and m temperatures), a substantial reduction against mn connection weights in the usual learning scheme. So the generalization capability of the model should be improved substantially.

7.3 COMPUTATIONAL EXPERIMENTS

7.3.1 Handwritten Digits

The handwritten-digit classifiers have been trained by both of the following:

1. The original training set of 1000 samples of each digit (i.e., a total of 10,000 samples)
2. A reduced training set of 100 samples of each digit (i.e., a total of 1000 samples).

The classifiers have been applied to data transformed to 20 features found by the supervised feature-discovery algorithm of Section 7.2. The misclassification rates for linear classifiers are given in Tables 7.1 and 7.2 for backpropagation classifiers with 5, 10, 20, and 40 hidden units in Tables 7.3 and 7.4.

Compared with classifying noncompressed data, supervised feature discovery brought about improvement in test set performance, in particular if the reduced training set has been used. As for unsupervised feature discovery, this indicates improved generalization. On the other hand, it has been surprising that no substantial perfor-

TABLE 7.1 Handwritten Digits: Misclassification Rates (Percent)[a]

	Noncompressed	20 Features
Full set	1.29	5.82
Reduced set	0.00	1.90

[a]Supervised feature discovery, linear classifiers. Results for training set.

TABLE 7.2 Handwritten Digits: Misclassification Rates (Percent)[a]

	Noncompressed	20 Features
Full set	5.55	6.65
Reduced set	14.70	10.13

[a]Supervised feature discovery, linear classifiers. Results for test set.

TABLE 7.3 Handwritten Digits: Misclassification Rates (Percent)[a]

	Hidden Units	Noncompressed	20 Features
Full set	5	3.57	6.24
	10	0.04	4.63
	20	0.00	2.84
	40	0.00	1.32
Reduced set	5	0.00	0.46
	10	0.00	0.00
	20	0.00	0.00
	40	0.00	0.00

[a]Supervised feature discovery, nonlinear linear classifiers. Results for training set.

TABLE 7.4 Handwritten Digits: Misclassification Rates (Percent)[a]

	Hidden Units	Noncompressed	20 Features
Full set	5	9.48	8.50
	10	5.35	5.88
	20	3.73	5.23
	40	2.53	5.55
Reduced set	5	17.36	12.40
	10	10.47	11.07
	20	8.53	10.51
	40	7.38	10.59

[a]Supervised feature discovery, nonlinear linear classifiers. Results for test set.

mance gain could be attained compared with unsupervised feature discovery. While training set results for supervised feature discovery combined with linear and five-hidden-unit classifiers are partially significantly better, training set results for higher numbers of hidden units are significantly worse. The relation is even less satisfactory for test results.

A possible explanation is that convergence to network parameters preserving the maximum of input variance is disturbed substantially by the term optimizing the features for the given task. An improvement of this convergence may be a topic for further study. If they do not succeed, the only possible conclusion is that unsupervised feature discovery is the right way.

7.3.2 Thyroid Data

As for the unsupervised feature discovery, some initial experiments with a reduced thyroid data set, 360 records from the 1985 set and 360 from the 1986, have been performed (Hrycej [76]). On this reduced data set, supervised feature discovery generalized substantially better than did other two-layer models.

However, as in Chapter 5, the performance of supervised feature discovery on the full thyroid data set has been poor. Once more, this can be explained by (1) the high nonlinearity of the problem and (2) weak dependencies between individual input variables.

7.4 RELATED WORK

There are plenty of approaches that can be viewed as instances of the present concept of finding first features or other transformations of input and subsequently applying a supervised learning algorithm to it. In some cases, the second phase becomes trivial. For example, it may consist of a conjunctive or disjunctive connection of the features or clusters found by the first phase.

One such approach is the learning algorithm of Valiant [156] for arbitrary Boolean functions. This algorithm, which may apply to machine learning rather than to neural networks, starts with a repository of disjunctions of inputs (each conjunction corresponding to a hidden unit) and filters out those inconsistent with learning examples. The output unit is simply a conjunction of such hidden units. In this way, an arbitrary Boolean function in the conjunctive normal form can be learned in polynomial time. Other algorithms for learning disjunctions of conjunctions have been proposed by Valiant [157] and Hampson and Volper [58].

Another instance is the vector quantization algorithm of Kohonen et al. [92]. Instead of quantizing the entire input space by Kohonen maps [91], it quantizes the input space for each class separately. So it tries to model and separate the regions for individual classes. After a certain number of clusters (corresponding to individual hidden units) are found for each class, the clusters for one class are disjunctively connected in the output layer.

A more sophisticated algorithm has been proposed by Poggio and Girosi [128]. This algorithm finds a problem-independent representation in the hidden layer and uses the optimal MSE linear classifier in the output layer. The hidden layer uses radial basis functions (instead of sigmoid functions), which are formally very similar to the competitive activation functions of Kohonen maps used in the vector quantization algorithm. An interesting feature of this algorithm is that it is based on explicit optimization of smoothness and generalization properties of the functional represented by the neural network, using the results of the regularization theory.

One of the first neural network classification algorithms is the RCU algorithm of Reilly et al. [130]. This algorithm is performing quantization of class regions by sequential search through, and adaptation to, training patterns. It can be viewed as a heuristic predecessor of the vector quantization algorithm. The goal of improving the convergence of backpropagation learning has been pursued explicitly by Orfanidis [117]. The improvement is reached by orthogonalization of data in each layer by a Gram–Schmidt preprocessor.

An interesting network inversion algorithm for extraction of *characteristic features of a given class*, instead of those of a given *classification task* has been presented by Linden and Kindermann [101]. In a network inversion task, an input vector is searched for which produces an output that is the closest to a given target output for a given network. This can be done by a gradient descent in a similar manner as for backpropagation learning. The difference is that the derivatives are taken with regard to the network input, instead of with regard to the network weights. If additional constraints penalizing the magnitude of input activation are introduced into the objective function, the algorithm finds input values that are the most significant for producing the given output.

7.5 SUPERVISED FEATURE DISCOVERY AND ADAPTIVE RESONANCE THEORY

The supervised feature discovery of Section 7.4 has been formulated as a unidirectional process in two steps: (1) extracting features optimal for the given task, and (2) supervised learning. This sequential procedure has been chosen because of its simplicity and modularity.

However, it is also conceivable to perform both steps in parallel. The necessity of parallelism is particularly strong in an interactive real-time learning mode. A rudimentary form of such parallel supervised feature discovery takes place during backpropagation learning—hidden units can be expected to be assigned to emergent features.

A much more ambitious attempt to implement interactive learning has been accomplished by Grossberg in his adaptive resonance theory [50]. A brief overview of this theory is given in Section 2.5.5. Although adaptive resonance theory is an unsupervised learning procedure and its goals are different from those of supervised feature discovery, it provides important insights into the feature discovery process.

Particularly interesting is its relationship to the findings of developmental psychology. In the next subsections we discuss this topic briefly.

7.5.1 Piaget's Assimilation and Accommodation

In Chapter 1 of this book, Piaget's theory of developmental stages was quoted as an argument in favor of modular learning. There is also another important part of Piaget's work that is relevant to the topic of this book: the theory of assimilation and accommodation. According to Piaget [125], patterns are not simply memorized and associated with other patterns. Rather than this, new associations arise by the interaction of two principles.

- *Assimilation* is the process of integration of new patterns into the existing structures. It leads to *strengthening* of these structures. In the early ontogenetic stages of human development such structures may be inborn reflexes. In the later stages, the structures to which new patterns are assimilated are much more complex—they are constituted by the totality of concepts so far acquired. The role of assimilation is the *interpretation* of new patterns in the light of the existing structure.

- *Accommodation* is the process of modification of existing structures by new patterns. A typical behavior related to accommodation is mimicking. Accommodation is responsible for *optimization* of performance during the development.

Adaptation is a balanced interaction between both components. An overemphasised assimilation leads to egocentric, nonadaptive behavior. A harmful effect of excessive accommodation is instability.

The concepts of assimilation and accommodation can be applied to adaptive pattern recognition.

- Assimilation corresponds to assigning patterns to categories and improving the definition of the corresponding category.
- Accommodation can be viewed as changing the category system of the classifier on arrival of completely novel patterns.

The problem of keeping balance between assimilation and accommodation can also be viewed as a reformulation of the stability–plasticity dilemma, that is, of the problem of how to learn new things without forgetting knowledge acquired previously.

7.5.2 Assimilation and Accommodation by Adaptive Resonance

It is exactly the approach of Section 7.5.1 that was adopted by Grossberg [50] and later by Carpenter and Grossberg [24] in their adaptive resonance theory (ART). Let us recall the basic scheme of ART (Figure 7.3).

A simplified version of the algorithm (Lippmann [102]) can be characterized by the following formulas.

- *Pattern recognition* is done by computing matching scores for pattern vector **x** and bottom-up weight vectors $\mathbf{b}_j$:

$$\mu_j = \sum_i b_{ij}(t)x_i. \qquad (7.7)$$

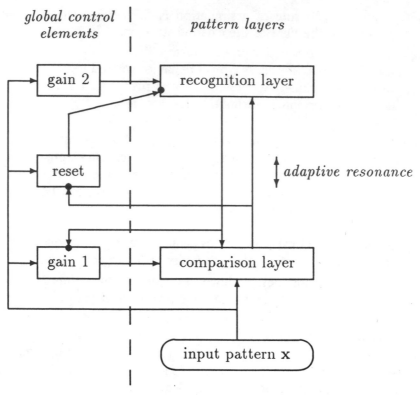

Figure 7.3. *Adaptive resonance theory network. Inhibitory connections are in-dicated by filled circles.*

The recognition layer unit with the highest score is selected. It represents the category of the pattern.

- *Assimilation* takes place if the similarity of the pattern with the top-down weight vector t_j of the selected recognition layer unit

$$\frac{\sum_i t_{ij} x_i}{\sum_i x_i} \tag{7.8}$$

exceeds a threshold ρ called vigilance. It consists of changing the top-down weights by

$$t_{ij}(t+1) = t_{ij}(t)x_i \tag{7.9}$$

and the bottom-up weights by

$$b_{ij}(t+1) = \frac{t_{ij}(t)x_i}{0.5 + \sum_i t_{ij}(t)x_i}. \tag{7.10}$$

So the category corresponding to the selected recognition layer unit assimilates the pattern **x**.

- *Accommodation* takes place if the similarity (7.7) is below the vigilance threshold ρ. In this case the structure of the category system is modified: A new processing unit is added to the recognition layer. Its weights are set equal to the pattern **x**.

CHAPTER 8 ⎯⎯⎯⎯⎯⎯⎯⎯⎯⎯

Decomposition of the Represented Mapping

Supervised feature discovery represents an attempt to decompose the mapping materialized by a neural network in a vertical way. In a mathematical formalism, this would correspond to a decomposition into a feature extraction function nested in an output function.

Another possibility is obviously a horizontal decomposition, for example, into a sum of different functions. This is usual in classical approaches to functional approximation. A mapping is approximated by a sum of predefined distinct (typically, orthogonal) functions.

A surprising property of neural networks with sigmoid hidden units is that they are capable of nonlinear functional approximation using a set of the *same* (i.e., sigmoid) functions. (Similar properties are exhibited by the radial basis function.) On the other side, the fact that all functions are sigmoid reduces the possibilities (and the sense) of horizontal decomposition for purely nonlinear approximation problems.

However, few problems are purely nonlinear. In particular, many classification problems turn out to be linear or nearly linear. (For arguments supporting this thesis, see Section 6.3.) By "nearly linear" I mean problems for which the optimal misclassification rate is only slightly lower than the misclassification rate attainable by a linear classifier. Anyway, we can expect that a certain number of sigmoid hidden units are wasted for linear separation. The use of linear functions for linear separation is certainly preferable to the use of sigmoid units for the same goal, since sigmoid units have to "discover" the linearity (by making their weights small). This discovery is always connected with computational expense. So it seems to make sense to decompose a classification or mapping problem horizontally into a linear and a nonlinear part.

8.1 DECOMPOSITION INTO LINEAR AND NONLINEAR PARTS

The topology of a corresponding neural network is given in Figure 8.1. The linear module of the classifier consists of direct connec-

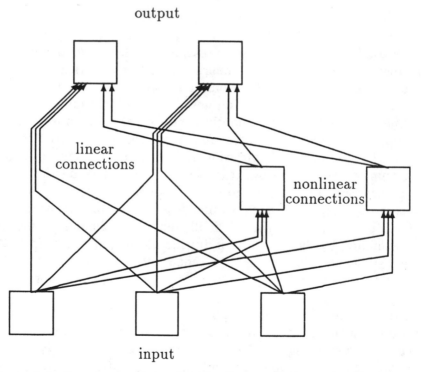

Figure 8.1. *Neural network topology for* linear + nonlinear *classifiers. Linear part, direct connections between input and output layer; nonlinear part, connections via hidden layer.*

tions from the input to the output units. The nonlinear module is implemented by an inserted hidden layer and its connections. The mapping represented by the network can be formally written as

$$y_j = \sum_i u_{ji}x_i + \sum_k w_{jk}sig\left(\sum_i v_{ji}x_i\right). \qquad (8.1)$$

Both linear and nonlinear modules can be trained simultaneously, a more modular approach is to let the linear part converge to an optimum, freeze its weights, and train the nonlinear part.

8.2 COMPUTATIONAL EXPERIMENTS

The hypothesis of Section 8.1 has been that a certain number of hidden units is engaged in linear separation, while the linear separation task can be more efficiently solved by a linear classifier. A practical consequence of this hypothesis would be that adding a linear module, some hidden units can be economized.

The following computational experiments have been performed to verify this thesis. Optimal classification performance for thyroid data has been reached with two or three hidden units (see computational experiments of Section 5), so there is no saving potential in the hidden layer for this data set. This is why only the handwritten-digit data set has been considered.

8.2.1 Handwritten Digits

A series of runs with two types of classifiers has been run:

1. A conventional network with a single hidden layer of 5, 10, 20, and 40 sigmoid hidden units
2. A modular network with the topology given in Figure 8.1, with the same numbers of hidden units

In both cases, loss functions of Section 6.3 have been used. The results for training and test sets (full sets of 10,000 records each) are given in Tables 8.1 and 8.2.

For the training set, the following conclusions can be made:

TABLE 8.1   Handwritten Digits: Misclassification Rates (Percent)[a]

	Hidden Units	Noncompressed	20 Features	40 Features
Nonlinear	5	3.57	8.39	6.15
	10	0.04	3.27	1.93
	20	0.00	1.33	0.05
	40	0.00	0.78	0.01
Linear + nonlinear	5	0.17	4.11	2.03
	10	0.00	3.51	0.80
	20	0.00	1.17	0.05
	40	0.00	0.66	0.02

[a]Nonlinear versus linear + nonlinear classifiers, results for training set.

TABLE 8.2   Handwritten Digits: Misclassification Rates (Percent)[a]

	Hidden Units	Noncompressed	20 Features	40 Features
Full set	5	9.48	8.94	7.32
	10	5.35	4.35	4.14
	20	3.73	3.68	3.34
	40	2.53	3.36	2.77
Reduced set	5	5.47	5.09	4.43
	10	6.12	4.46	3.80
	20	4.77	3.20	3.76
	40	3.98	3.14	3.33

[a]Nonlinear versus linear + nonlinear classifiers, results for test set.

1. The performance of modular classifiers is monotonically better than that of conventional ones with corresponding numbers of hidden units.
2. Conventional classifiers with 10 hidden units are roughly equivalent to modular ones with five hidden units. Linear classifier seems to save five hidden units.
3. The superiority of modular classifiers is particularly clear for lower numbers of hidden units and diminishes with their growing number.

For the test set, analogous conclusions are valid only for five and 10 hidden units. For 20 and 40 hidden units, a deterioration of classification performance can be observed. This is rather surprising—

adding an infinitely smooth (in the sense of having a zero second derivative) linear function could be expected to improve generalization. Obviously, a further study going beyond the scope of this book is necessary.

8.3 LINEAR CLASSIFIER AS A LEARNING MODULE

Let us now briefly turn to the engineering effect of the decomposition of a neural classifier into a linear and a nonlinear part. It is, in fact, very simple. The performance of the linear module is measured by the same criterion as that of the whole classifier: by the misclassification rate. The most important benefits are the following:

- The convergence of linear module is relatively fast and theoretically guaranteed (see Section 6.3).
- The performance (i.e., the misclassification rate) of the linear module is the lower limit for the performance of the whole classifier. This is obvious since the nonlinear part must be better than no classifier. This trivial observation is helpful in preventing us from terminating the training too early—the nonlinear part starts doing its job only after the misclassification rate of the entire classifier passed that of the linear module.

CHAPTER 9 ⸻⸻⸻⸻

Decomposing the Network to Minimize Interactions

The approaches presented so far have been based on a decomposition of the learning procedure into modules with different functionalities. The learning task has been viewed as a sequence of subtasks with different relationship to the overall objective of learning. By contrast, in this chapter we view the learning task as monolithic as far as its objective function is concerned. It follows a well-known approach of systems theory that consists in decomposing a complex system in a way such that the interactions between the parts are minimal. We view the task of learning neural network weights as a complex system of elementary subtasks each of which consists of learning a single weight.

In the next sections, an analysis of interactions between individual weights is done and an algorithm based on this analysis is designed (see also Hrycej [77]).

9.1 INTERACTIONS BETWEEN THE WEIGHTS OF A MULTILAYER NETWORK

The basic formula of error backpropagation (using the denotation of Rumelhart et al. [139]) is

$$\frac{dE}{dw_{ji}} = \frac{dE}{do_j}\frac{do_j}{dnet_j}\frac{dnet_j}{dw_{ji}}$$

$$= \frac{dE}{do_j}f'(net_j)o_i$$

$$= (t_j - o_j)f'(net_j)o_i \qquad \text{for the output layer}$$

$$= \sum_k \frac{dE}{do_k}\frac{do_k}{dnet_k}w_{kj}f'(net_j)o_i \qquad \text{for hidden layers}$$

$$(9.1)$$

To simplify the analysis, let us assume that hidden units are linear. This allows us to omit the derivative $f'(net_j) = o_j(1 - o_j)$. So we get a kind of lower bound of interactions that will be valid in the middle, nearly linear part of sigmoid units.

Under this simplifying assumption, we can express the derivative (9.1) as a sum of products of individual weights. The output o_j of a kth layer unit contributes by k factors to this product. For the jth layer of a network with K layers of connections (i.e., an index refers to the layer's units and its input connections, while input units do not count to any layer), each product contains

- K such factors in the expression for output units o_K [see formula (9.1) for the output layer where the recursion starts]
- $K - j$ factors resulting from recursive applications of (9.1) to get dE/dw_{ji}
- $j - 1$ factors in the expression for the activation of the $(j - 1)$th unit [o_i in (9.1)].

In other words, the value of each derivative dE/dw_{ji} depends on $2K - 1$ factors. Changing the weights of all layers simultaneously is consistent with the theory of gradient method as long as the learning rate is infinitesimally small. However, it is not the case if higher learning rates are used. The reason for this is that the direction of change has been computed under the condition of unchanged (or only infinitesimally changed) remaining weights. This maximum-gradient direction can then be substantially disturbed by changing remaining weights simultaneously.

On the other hand, using higher learning rates is vital for convergence speed. An extreme solution to the interdependency problem would be to change a single weight at a time. But the speed gain from a higher learning rate would certainly get lost by the fact that gradients would have to be recomputed after each single-weight change. So it would be desirable to find groups of weights within which the interferences are low. For obvious reasons, linear (i.e., additive) interferences are less harmful than nonlinear (e.g., multiplicative) interferences.

This can be accomplished if we observe the factors in the expression for error derivative. From these factors, only a single one (the one necessary for computing the activation of output unit) represents a weight of the same (i.e., the jth) layer. Consequently, defining a layer as a learning module would result in reducing the order of expression for the derivative with regard to the output error from $2K - 1$ to 1. If we partitioned the network vertically, across the layers, we would not diminish the order at all.

This analysis indicates that chaining the weights of all layers simultaneously produces highly nonlinear interferences between the changing weights. A logical proposal is then to *modify only the weights of a single layer at a time*.

9.2   LAYER-BY-LAYER MODIFICATION OF THE BACKPROPAGATION ALGORITHM

An iteration of the learning algorithm proposed here consists of a sequence of learning phases for individual layers. Each layer's weights are learned while other layers' weights remain constant.

A special property of the output layer is that its units need not be nonlinear. While nonlinearity of hidden units is a necessary condition for the network to be capable of learning nonlinear mappings, nonlinear (e.g., sigmoid) units in the output layer do not bring about any obvious advantage:

- If the network is used for classification, the output unit with the maximal activation represents the estimated class. So the outcome is not influenced by a sigmoid (or any other increasing) transformation.

- If the network is used for modeling an input–output mapping (e.g., forecasts), linear units are more universal than sigmoid units because their range is $(-\infty, \infty)$, that of sigmoid units being $\langle 0, 1 \rangle$.

On the contrary, an important advantage of linear output units is that the optimal weights of connections entering the output layer can be computed exactly with the help of the linear regression formula

$$W = C_{xy} C_{xx}^{-1} \tag{9.2}$$

with C_{xx} and C_{xy} the covariance matrices. Since the number of hidden units is typically quite low, the computational complexity of the matrix inversion plays no significant role, and the results are substantially better than when using the linear form of the delta rule (Widrow and Hoff [170]).

For a three-layer network, which currently seems to be the one used most frequently in practical applications, the learning algorithm is the following (with V the matrix of weights between the input and hidden layers and W the matrix of weights between the hidden layer and the output layer):

For *a certain number of iterations* **do**

1. Perform one or a fixed number of backpropagation learning epochs for V, keeping W constant.
2. Compute a hidden-layer activation vector **h** for each input pattern (by forward propagation via V).
3. Determine the optimal weight matrix W for mapping of hidden-layer vectors **h** to desired outputs.

9.3 COMPUTATIONAL EXPERIENCE

The hypothesis that layer-by-layer learning should perform better than nonmodular backpropagation for higher learning rates will now be verified by computational experiments.

TABLE 9.1   Thyroid Data: Misclassification Rates (Percent)[a]

Learning Rate	100 Iterations	300 Iterations	1000 Iterations
0.01	6.4	5.1	3.4
0.03	5.8	4.7	3.2
0.10	5.3	4.2	4.1
0.30	6.9	5.2	5.4
1.00	22.7	42.2	43.8

[a]Conventional backpropagation, results for test set.

TABLE 9.2   Thyroid Data: Misclassification Rates (Percent)[a]

Learning Rate	100 Iterations	300 Iterations	1000 Iterations
0.01	5.8	4.3	3.7
0.03	5.1	3.3	2.9
0.10	3.2	2.7	2.1
0.30	2.7	2.1	2.1
1.00	2.3	2.2	2.1

[a]Layer-by-layer backpropagation, results for test set.

9.3.1   Thyroid Data

For thyroid data, both models have been run with various learning rates: 0.01, 0.03, 0.1, 0.3, and 1.0. The results are given in Tables 9.1 and 9.2. Regarding these results, obvious conclusions are:

1. Layer-by-layer backpropagation delivers significantly better results for all learning rates.
2. Layer-by-layer backpropagation allows high learning rates and thus faster convergence.
3. While conventional backpropagation converged really well only for the learning rate of 0.03, and diverged for learning rates above 0.03, layer-by-layer backpropagation worked almost equally well for all parameter values.

9.3.2   Handwritten Digits

Several test runs with handwritten digits have been run, too. As for thyroid data, the layer-by-layer algorithm has been superior to conventional backpropagation. However, the performance of both has been rather poor in comparison with the algorithms of previous sections (test set error rates about 10%). The reason for this is that the layer-by-layer algorithm necessarily uses mean-squared error as the error criterion; otherwise, the output layer weights could not be computed by formula (9.2). This is a considerable disadvantage vis-à-vis algorithms that can use loss functions (see Chapter 6) as successfully as mean-squared error.

So although the performance of the layer-by-layer learning algorithm may be good for classification problems such as the thyroid diagnostics, its preferred domain of application should be learning continuous mappings (e.g., in signal processing or system identification), where mean-squared error as the error measure is the proper choice.

9.4 RELATED WORK

An interesting approach to learning layer by layer has been pursued by Shepanski [146]. His work has been motivated by the intention to apply the optimal estimation theory for determining optimal weights rather than by an analysis of interactions in gradient learning.

For a network with one hidden layer and weight matrices V and W, his algorithm is as follows:

Step 1: Initiate the matrix V randomly.

Step 2: For all input patterns x_k, compute the corresponding hidden-layer patterns y_k (received by passing the elements of vector $V x_k$ through the sigmoid function).

Step 3: For hidden-layer patterns y_k and desired output patterns z_k, compute the optimal linear mapping matrix W by (9.2).

Step 4: For each desired output pattern z_k, compute the hidden-layer pattern y_k such that $(z_k - W y_k)^2$ is minimal. There are three different cases, depending on the relationship between the number of output units j and the number of hidden units h:

1. For $h = j$, y_k is determined exactly as $W^{-1} z_k$. The error $(z_k - W y_k)^2$ is zero.

2. For $h > j$, there are infinitely many solutions such that $(z_k - W y_k)^2$ is zero. The solution with a minimal norm is received by the underconstrained pseudoinverse of W.

3. For $h < j$, solution with a minimum error $(z_k - W y_k)^2$ is received by the overconstrained pseudoinverse of W.

Step 5: Since the individual components of the vectors y_k do not generally fall into the interval $\langle 0, 1 \rangle$, they are rescaled. (Otherwise, they would not be able to be generated as outputs from sigmoid hidden units.)

Step 6: Each rescaled hidden-layer vector is passed through an inverse sigmoid function to get a desired vector of inputs into the hidden units inp_k.

Step 7: The matrix V of connection weights between the input layer and the hidden layer is computed analogously to Step 3.

Step 8: Steps 2 and 3 are repeated to get an optimal matrix W.

An indisputable advantage of this algorithm is that it is based primarily on exact algorithms of estimation theory. However, it cannot claim to be an exact algorithm for computing optimal weights. (This claim has not been made by its author.) The reason for this lies in the heuristic nature of Steps 5 and 6. It is also difficult to evaluate the contribution of Steps 3 and 7 to the global optimality. Even if the algorithm is made iterative (over Steps 2 to 7), it is not clear under which conditions the algorithm converges to a global optimum rather than only to local optima. At first glance, its chances for this are not higher than those for the gradient method.

On the other hand, its convergence speed may be superior to that of the gradient method. Its other advantage may be the absence of parameters such as the learning rate of the momentum term weight. Shepanski [146] presents results of computational experiments from the signal processing domain showing an impressive performance gain against the backpropagation algorithm. However, only 60 backpropagation iterations have been performed, which in my experience is hardly a sufficient number.

The results of my own computational experiments with this algorithm on thyroid data have been disappointing. Even with its iterative version, the algorithm generated a set of relatively bad weights (misclassification rates over 6%) and never escaped from this state. The problem seems to arise from the low variability of desired outputs in classification problems—there are as few different outputs as there are classes. So in Steps 5 and 6, only three different hidden-layer vectors can be generated. So the entire classification task is

concentrated in Step 7 and thus becomes a task of linear discriminant analysis. However, the idea of the algorithm is certainly very
interesting and worth further testing and development.

CHAPTER 10 —————————————

Modularizing the Application Task

Until now, we have focused on modularization approaches that focused on learning phases in general. However, from the engineering point of view, the most natural approach is to look for decomposition cues in the application task itself. Such an approach can be expected to work particularly well since application tasks generally exhibit considerable structuredness. In particular, (1) tasks may consist of relatively independent subtasks, and (2) the solution may be found by successive refinement.

This topic has barely been mentioned in the neural network literature. The goal of the present section is to address this decomposition approach. In contrast to previous chapters, the approaches could not be verified by computational experiments. There have been two reasons for this omission.

1. The classification problems used throughout this book, thyroid diagnosis and handwritten-digit recognition, represent relatively structureless tasks. The classification of thyroid disorders as well as that of handwritten digits is interesting only as a whole. It is of limited use to separate the digit subset $0, 1, 2, 3, 4$ from $5, 6, 7, 8, 9$. Even if separating digit subclasses were a helpful preprocessing step for increasing the efficiency of learning to sep-

arate all individual digits (see Section 10.3), there would be too many such possible subclasses. To test which of them are appropriate to improve learning would be an interesting but very time consuming task.

2. There is hardly any theory that could be followed and verified by such computational experiments. This would make the results rather arbitrary and of limited use.

This chapter is organized as follows. Section 10.1 is concerned with mapping the task structure to the network topology. The approach presented in Section 10.2 goes one step further: It assigns to each subtask a complete network. The topic of Section 10.3 is the possibility of learning in successive phases, corresponding to steps of task solution. Section 10.4 is an introduction to the vision of interacting neural networks.

10.1 DECOMPOSING NETWORK STRUCTURE ACCORDING TO TASK

The simplest principle of task-oriented problem decomposition is to assign a part of the network to a subtask. Since it is difficult to imagine a "part" of a classification, this approach will be illustrated on a control problem.

Let us have a plant whose dynamics can be described by the following two differential equations:

$$a\ddot{x} + k\ddot{y} = u$$
$$k\ddot{x} + \ddot{y} + 2dw\dot{y} + w^2 y = 0, \tag{10.1}$$

with a, k, w, and d being constants. This could be, for example, a description of a single-coordinate dynamics of a nonrigid body with damping coefficient d. The position of the body is given by x. The variable u corresponds to a force or torque exerted to the the body. Since the body is nonrigid, the force u induces oscillations described their first modal coordinate y.

The goal is to to determine the controller action u as a function of measured values x, $\dot{x}$, y, and $\dot{y}$ to keep the value of x as close as

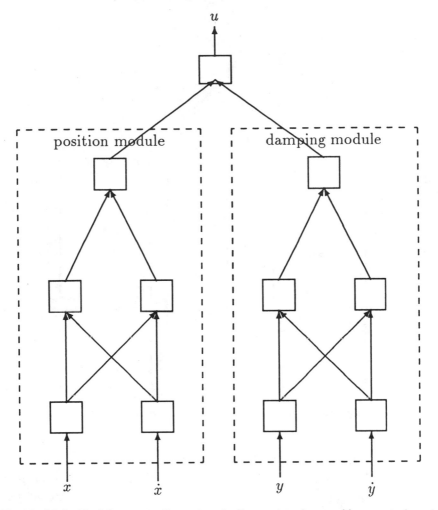

Figure 10.1. *Modular controller network. Two subtasks, position control and damping, are assigned two subnetworks.*

possible to zero. Simultaneously, it is desirable to keep the oscillations as weak as possible, first, because they may be harmful to the body, and second, because they would disturb the stabilization of the body in the zero position. Obviously, the task has two parts:

1. Bringing the body to the zero position as quickly as possible if a deviation occurs.
2. Active damping of oscillations.

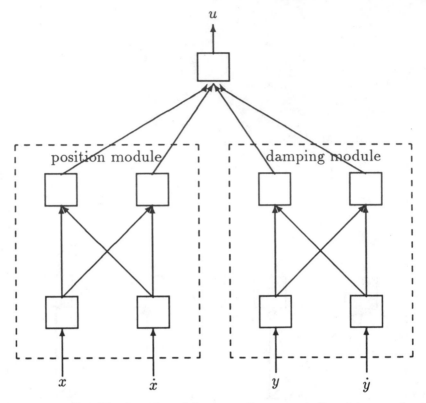

Figure 10.2. *Simplification of modular controller network. Special case of additive outputs of both subnetworks.*

A modular network topology for this task is shown in Figure 10.1. The first module is a position control module. It consists of two input units assigned to to x and $\dot{x}$ measurements, and two hidden units. The second module is an oscillation damping module. Its inputs are y and $\dot{y}$, and it also contains two hidden units. Each module produces an output, and the control action u is a sum of the outputs. If output units of both modules and the integrating output unit u are all additive, the topology of Figure 10.1 can be reduced to that of Figure 10.2.

It should be pointed out that such decomposition is correct only if the "partial actions," the position control action and the oscillation damping action, are additive. Practical experiments have confirmed this hypothesis for the given model, but it may not be the case else-

`where. The general procedure for this type of decomposition can be formulated in the following way:

1. Appropriate subtasks (e.g., position control and oscillation damping) are identified.
2. For each subtask, necessary inputs to the corresponding module (e.g., x and $\dot{x}$ for the position control module) are determined.
3. An appropriate number of hidden units is assigned to each module (two to each module in the example of Figure 10.1). This number should be proportional to the expected degree of difficulty of the subtask.
4. The type of summarizing the outputs from all modules is defined (e.g., addition).

This approach has been pursued by Graham and D'Eleuterio [47]. Their application comes from the robotic control domain. The plant is a rigid manipulation with rotary joints. Its dynamics to be modeled can be described in the form

$$\mu(\sigma, \ddot{\sigma}) + \eta(\sigma, \dot{\sigma}) = f \qquad (10.2)$$

σ being the angle and f the torque exerted. The first term, $\mu(\sigma, \ddot{\sigma})$, represents the rate-linear component of the mapping. The second term, $\eta(\sigma, \dot{\sigma})$, corresponds to the nonlinear component.

This decomposition of mapping leads to a decomposition of the task of learning this mapping. This, in turn, suggests a corresponding decomposition of the network into two modules. Graham and D'Eleuterio used the CMAC network of Albus [4, 5], in which the two modules are trained simultaneously. They reported a considerable reduction in both mapping error and the number of samples required for training. For related work, see the references in [47].

10.2 USING MULTIPLE SUBTASK NETWORKS

The previous approach was concerned with assigning each subtask *a part* of the network. This makes possible the use of a single neural network model and the learning algorithm for the entire structured network. The cost for this convenience is a limitation on the variability of subtasks. All subtasks must be of the same basic type (e.g., all subtasks may be control problems solved by the same learning algorithm).

The approach described in this section is one step more general. It turns each subtask into an individual neural network problem with its own interface, model, and learning algorithm. This freedom makes the scope of the approach broader, but also requires more manual coordination. The inputs and outputs into the individual subtask network modules have to be carefully defined. All modules are then usually embedded into an application software package that is responsible for the communication between modules, possible algorithmic branching, and further algorithmic components.

An example of this approach is the two-stage architecture of Lefebvre, Nicolas, and Degoul [100] for acoustic signal classification. In the first stage, a multilayer perceptron network is used to classify the signals into the following classes: (1) transient sounds, (2) surrounding noise, and (3) quasi-stationary noise. For each class, class-specific preprocessing is done, after which, class-specific classifiers are used.

10.3   DECOMPOSING THE TASK INTO SUCCESSIVE PHASES

In Section 10.2 we were concerned with a topological network decomposition according to subtasks. Another, independent question is that of assignment of successive learning phases to these subtasks. An extreme approach would be to train each module separately to do its task and to expect the entire modular architecture to perform well in the overall task. Although this is theoretically possible, it would work well only if individual subtasks do not exhibit any interferences. For example, the oscillation damping of the example in Section 10.2 would have to be completely independent of the position control. This can scarcely be guaranteed.

A less extreme approach is the incremental one. After a subtask has been learned by the corresponding module, one more module is added and the entire architecture is trained for the subtask assigned to it, together with all subtasks learned previously. If the subtasks are ordered by difficulty, we receive a typically human learning approach: first, learning simple tasks, and then, incrementally improving the skill by adding new facets of the overall task.

In the classification domain, this approach amounts, first, to separating some subsets of all classes (instead of separating the individual classes immediately), and further, to splitting these subsets down into single classes. This is closely related to several models in the field of machine learning, one of the most prominent models of this type being the CART model of Breiman et al. [19]. They propose constructing a tree in each node of which the set of training patterns is split into two subsets. This split is to be optimal with regard to an entropy within both subsets; this entropy is low if the subset contains instances of only a few classes. So the algorithm implicitly searches for class partitionings advantageous for further learning.

Although application of the incremental learning principles to classification may seem artificial, their application to control problems is frequently quite natural. Let us consider the nonrigid body control discussed in the preceding section. The goal is position control, but with simultaneous oscillation damping. The position control task is substantially easier for a rigid body. The dynamics of a rigid body of mass equivalent to that described by equations (10.1) is given by a simple relationship:

$$a\ddot{x} = u \tag{10.3}$$

So the goal of the first learning stage may be to learn the position control of this equivalent rigid body. The second learning stage is then concerned with the more difficult problem of position control of a flexible body. A more sophisticated approach may consist of gradually decreasing the rigidness of the body by decreasing the value of damping coefficient d in (10.3).

10.4 INTERACTING NEURAL NETWORKS

With the growing complexity of intelligent systems, explicit coordination of individual subsystems becomes difficult—in some cases even intractable. On the other hand, the very substance of human intelligence seems to consist of a perfect coordination of many relatively independent functions. Individual subsystems and functional circuits of the human neural system can perform their functions simultaneously and are robust against disturbances of one function by another.

For example, an experienced bike driver can hold a bag in one hand without disturbing his or her balance and without a substantial loss of ability to steer the bike. He or she simply substitutes the occupied subsystem (one hand) by a more extensive use of the other subsystem (the other hand) to solve the balancing task, even though it is modified by shifting the center of gravity to the side where the bag is held.

A more hierarchical system seems to be involved in tasks such as walking. Higher-level activities such as walking in a certain direction are pursued persistently even if the conditions (e.g., slope, obstacles) vary considerably and necessitate the activation of various muscular systems.

These and similar observations lead to the idea of artificial neural systems with interacting modules. An interesting approach has been taken by Beer [16], who constructed an artificial "computer cockroach," a simulated neural system capable of such higher behavioral patterns as exploratory behavior and feeding. The cockroach can choose appropriately between the two behavioral patterns, which use a common set of locomotion patterns, according to the actual environmental conditions, and modify them in a manner consistent with current preferences. The locomotion patterns, in turn, consist of coordinated lower-level patterns such as simplified muscle contractions of individual legs.

The most important result of this work is the empirical proof of the existence of complex *emergent behavior* of artificial neural network systems: A system composed of simplified constructs exhibits intelligent behavior beyond that deliberately encoded into the structure of the neural network. Although the robotic research of Brooks [20] does not explicitly concern neural networks, it is closely related to neural network systems such as that of Beer's computer cockroach. Brooks's robots are networks of communicating finite-state machines each of which is responsible for elementary higher- or lower-level locomotion tasks. This work presents further experimental evidence for emergent behavior. The fact that the two approaches are conceptually very similar, although arising from different disciplines, again makes obvious the necessity of interdisciplinary communication.

Important work from a related research field is that of Narendra and Thathachar [112] concerning learning automata. They present significant contributions to the theory of *interconnected automata* (see Section 2.7.5). Although learning automata are simpler constructs than entire neural networks, and thus the behavior of interconnected automata is simpler than that of interconnected neural networks, the theory of the former might become a good basis for the theory of the latter.

Decomposing Network Construction into Knowledge-Based and Learning Parts

So far, only decomposition of learning into parts that can themselves be solved by supervised or unsupervised learning has been considered. For an investigation of learning decomposition to be complete, the case of solving some parts of the learning task by nonlearning methods must also be considered briefly. Since learning can be characterized as extracting information from a set of training examples, nonlearning methods can be delineated as methods using information other than that contained in training examples. So *knowledge-based methods* using some type of explicit domain knowledge immediately appear to be candidates for nonlearning methods.

The next question to be solved is what part of the overall learning scheme can be supported by using explicit domain knowledge. It has been a common experience with expert system technology using numerical evaluations of probability or belief that human beings are weak in formulating hypotheses in numerical terms. Learning algorithms such as the gradient method seem to be clearly superior in appointing optimal numerical parameters. Consequently, it seems to make little sense to use explicit knowledge in determining *network parameters.* On the other hand, the chances for success in exploiting explicit knowledge for determining *network topology* appear to be considerably higher. Discussion of the possibility of decomposing learning into a topology design using explicit knowledge and determining optimal network parameters by some learning procedure is the subject of the present chapter.

11.1 NETWORK PARAMETERS VERSUS NETWORK TOPOLOGY

The neural networks considered so far have had a simple, predefined topology. For layered feedforward networks, this can be justified by the following facts:

1. For layered feedforward networks, the problem of network topology can be reduced to three subproblems:

    (a) The first subproblem is that of the *number of hidden layers*. Although there have been some investigations advocating the use of multiple hidden layers (e.g., Ho [67] or Le Cun et al. [99]), it has been my own experience during this and previous work that a single hidden-layer architecture is powerful enough for a great majority of practical tasks. This assumption seems so far to have been confirmed by the fact that the number of applications based on architectures with more than two hidden layers is negligible.

    (b) So far, the question of the optimal *number of hidden units* in the (single) hidden layer has not been given a theoretical answer. However, some number between the dimensionality of input and that of output always seems to be a good starting point. The optimal number can easily be determined by a few experiments.

    (c) The possibility of using networks with *incompletely connected* layers has been investigated by several researchers (e.g., Ji et al. [54]). This approach is also suggested by neurobiological findings. Although this research brought about many positive results, the efficiency gain is not always justified by the increased expense of the analysis necessary for pruning or prestructuring, at least with the present state of the art.

These arguments may suggest that research on network topology for layered feedforward networks is probably less rewarding than in the more general case of nonlayered feedback networks.

2. Even if we adopt the approach of this chapter and try to use explicit domain knowledge for an optimal topology design, feedforward layered networks are structurally too restricted to represent some real-world domain structure.

A consequence of these facts is that exploiting explicit knowledge to determine network topology has more chance for success if general, nonlayered neural networks are considered.

If the objective is to use both explicit knowledge and learning from examples cooperatively to solve a problem, it is necessary:

1. To find a knowledge representation paradigm based on graphs of sufficiently simple structure to be transformable to neural networks (one of the desirable properties would be the existence of a single-edge type).

2. To find an interpretation of network parameters within this knowledge representation paradigm.

3. To find an interpretation of neural network inference algorithms in the knowledge representation paradigm considered.

These are the topics of the following section.

11.2 RELATIONSHIP BETWEEN CAUSAL AND NEURAL NETWORKS

In artificial intelligence, several knowledge representation paradigms based on graphlike structures have been proposed. Some of them, such as semantic networks, use several types of edges, corresponding to several types of relations, but this is not the case for *dependency networks*. Some of these are out of consideration because they lack numerical parameters that can be learned. But a special type of probabilistic causal network called a *Bayesian network* (Pearl [120]) seems to be a particularly good candidate for isomorphy with neural networks.

Bayesian networks are based on representing causal influences by directed graphs and labeling the edges with conditional probabilities. Nodes whose instantiation is known are clamped to fixed truth values. A typical inference expected from Bayesian networks is the computation of probabilities of some logical statements given the available evidence. For networks of general topology and nontrivial size, an exact evaluation of such posterior probabilities for all nodes is computationally intractable. The only practically applicable procedure for this task is *stochastic simulation* (Pearl [122]). The stochastic character of this procedure and a network-oriented structure of Bayesian networks suggest a possible relationship to stochastic sampling procedures for neural networks such as Boltzmann machines.

A particularly general framework for stochastic sampling has been proposed by Geman and Geman [45]. These researchers have shown some essential properties of a simulation scheme called Gibbs sampling: in particular, *relaxation*, *annealing*, and *ergodicity*. The goal of this section is to show that Bayesian networks and their stochastic simulation are a special case of Gibbs sampling (see also Hrycej [78]). Establishing the relationship between Bayesian networks and models based on Gibbs sampling will provide relaxation-based connectionist models such as the Boltzmann machine with a probabilistic interpretation (see also Hrycej [79, 80]).

In Sections 6.2.2 and 6.2.3 we introduce Bayesian networks and the Gibbs sampling model, respectively. Section 6.2.4 shows the relationship between the two and how this relationship can be used to make statements about convergence and to find the most likely instantiation. In Section 6.2.5 we specialize to a well-known neural network model, the Boltzmann machine, and investigate its relationship to Gibbs sampling. In Section 6.2.6 we compare the approach presented here with related approaches.

11.2.1 Stochastic Simulation of Bayesian Networks

In this section we present a brief summary of Bayesian networks. For more details, see Pearl [120–123]. The notation is consistent with that of [122].

Bayesian networks are directed acyclic graphs whose nodes represent variables and whose edges represent causal influences (for a discussion of representational aspects, see Pearl and Verma [124]).

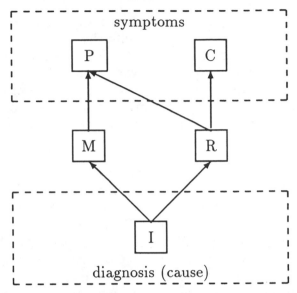

Figure 11.1. *Example: a Bayesian network. Meanings of nodes: I, influenza; R, infection of respiratory tract; M, muscle fatigue; P, reduced performance; C, cough attacks.*

An imaginary medical example of a Bayesian network is presented in Figure 11.1. For instance, the edge from "influenza" to "muscle fatigue" represents the statement "influenza *causes* muscle fatigue." The absence of edge between "reduced performance" and "cough attacks" means that there is no causal *direct* causal relationship between the two—the only relationship is via "infection of respiratory tract."

Definition 11.2.1 A **Bayesian network** is a quadruple $\{W, C, CP, E\}$, with W a set of nodes corresponding to variables, C a set of directed edges representing causality such that the directed graph $\{W, C\}$ is acyclic, CP a set of conditional probabilities $P(x \mid \mathbf{u}_x)$ for each variable X and each combination of the values of its parents $U_i \in U_x$ [or unconditional probabilities $P(x)$ for variables without parents], and E a set of clamped variables with fixed values, $E \subset W$.

Conditional probabilities $P(x \mid \mathbf{u}_x)$ express *expert knowledge* about the distribution of variable X conditioned on fixed values of its parent variables $\mathbf{u}_x$, on which X is causally dependent.

Note 11.2.1   In an acyclic network, it is always possible to index the variables in an ordering consistent with the orientation of network edges. The distribution of each variable is then conditioned only on its predecessors, that is, variables with a lower index. Under this condition a joint distribution of all variables is determined uniquely by the set CP of conditional probabilities from Definition 11.2.1 (the chain rule of [120, p. 244]. In other words, *any* complete set CP of a Bayesian network is consistent.

Throughout this chapter, the following notation for the variables of a Bayesian network will be used: Uppercase letters stand for variables and lowercase letters for their actual symbolic values as well as for their concrete truth values. So the symbol for the current value of a binary variable X is x, and this value may be either x (for x = true) or $\neg x$ (for x = false). Clamped variables, whose values are known in advance, express the available *evidence*. Arbitrary variables can be clamped whatever they represent, symptoms or diagnoses.

Like other artificial intelligence models, Bayesian networks are expected to allow useful *inference*. The inferential type typical for Bayesian networks is the *computation of posterior probabilities* of statements corresponding to nonclamped nodes, given the evidence expressed by clamped nodes. In the example of Figure 11.1, the probability of the diagnosis "influenza" could be questioned given the evidence "cough attacks" and "muscle fatigue." The fact that evidence can be clamped for any subset of diagnoses or symptoms makes it clear that computing posterior probabilities is (and must be) a *bidirectional* inference: Deducing symptoms from causes and diagnoses from symptoms must be possible.

Theorem 11.2.1   The joint posterior probability distribution of nonclamped variables from $W \backslash E$, conditioned on clamped variables from E, is given by

$$P(w \mid E) = \alpha \prod_i P(x_i \mid \mathbf{f}_i) \qquad (11.1)$$

with α a normalizing constant, $\mathbf{f}_i$ the values of parents of x_i and i ranging over all variables from W.

Proof. See Pearl [120].

Equation (11.1) represents an explicit relationship from which posterior probabilities for individual nonclamped variables could theoretically be computed. However, this is a difficult nonlinear computational problem. For networks of nontrivial size, it is computationally intractable except for some special topologies, such as trees or singly connected networks (see Pearl [119–121]). The only known pragmatic procedure for the general Bayesian network case is stochastic simulation (Pearl [122]), which can be performed by local operations on the network. The simulation uses the fact that the probability that variable X will have some value x depends solely on its parents, its children, and the parents of its children. This is stated formally by the following theorem.

Theorem 11.2.2   The probability distribution of each variable X in the network, conditioned on the state of all other variables, is given by the product

$$P(x \mid \mathbf{w}_x) = \alpha P(x \mid \mathbf{u}_x) \prod_j P[y_j \mid \mathbf{f}_j(x)] \qquad (11.2)$$

where α is a normalizing constant, independent of x, and x, $\mathbf{w}_x$, $\mathbf{u}_x$, y_j, and $\mathbf{f}_j(x)$ denote any consistent instantiations of X [$W_x = W \setminus - \{X\}$ (W being the set of all variables)], U_x (set of X's parents), Y_j (set of X's children), and F_j (set of parents of Y_j), respectively.

Proof. See [122].

Definition 11.2.2   Stochastic simulation of a Bayesian network is an algorithm that begins by setting nonclamped variables to arbitrary values and then iteratively performing the following steps:

Step 1: Choosing a nonclamped variable (in a fixed or random order encompassing all nonclamped variables).

Step 2: Computing its probability distribution (i.e., the probabilities of its being true or false) given the current values of neighbor variables according to Theorem 11.2.2.

Step 3: Taking a random sample from this distribution.

Step 4: Setting the variable to the value sampled.

There are two alternative methods for computing the posterior distribution of a variable:

- *Method A:* As a fraction of times the variable is true.
- *Method B*: As an average of the distributions of Step 2.

This iterative procedure is usually terminated after a certain stability of solution is reached.

11.2.2 Gibbs Sampling

Let us now approach the relationship between causal and neural networks from the neural side. Geman and Geman [45] have developed a very general framework for stochastic sampling on a graph structure with only local interactions between graph nodes: the *Markov random fields*. This sampling is called Gibbs sampling, after the probability distribution of variables in this graph structure (Gibbs distribution). Geman and Geman applied this theory to the restoration of noisy images. An application to systems of probabilistic constraints has been proposed by Geman [44]. It has turned out that this framework is also immediately applicable to stochastic neural network models such as the Boltzmann machine.

The theory is summarized briefly in this section. The reader interested in more details is referred to [45].

Definition 11.2.3 Gibbs distribution relative to a graph $\{S, G\}$, with S a set of nodes (or sites) s, to each of which corresponds a variable X_s, and G a neighborhood system, is a probability measure π on the space Ω of all variable values ω such that

$$\pi(\omega) = \frac{1}{Z} e^{-U(\omega)/T} \tag{11.3}$$

where Z is a normalizing constant,

$$Z = \int_\Omega e^{-U(\omega)/T} \, d\omega, \tag{11.4}$$

T a temperature constant, and U (the energy function or measure of constraint violation) is of the form

$$U(\omega) = \sum_{C \in \Theta} V_c(\omega) \tag{11.5}$$

with Θ being a set of all "cliques," that is, subgraphs of $\{S, G\}$ such that there is an edge for all pairs of its nodes.

Note 11.2.2   Gibbs sampling theory adopts the condition that the probability for any variable to assume each of its possible values is positive [45, p. 725]. This assumption rules out *logical* constraints between the variables—constraints forcing a variable to assume a certain value with probability 1 (and all other values with probability zero) given a certain combination of values of its neighbor variables. The zero probabilities of certain states would correspond to an infinite energy. Another manifestation of the same problem is that with zero probabilities for some value configurations, the joint probability cannot be expressed as a product of functions on the cliques (see [123, p. 135, Exercise 3.3*b*]) and thus violates the conditions of the theorem of Hammersley and Clifford ([17] or [123, p. 106]).

The following theorem concerns the distribution of a single variable X if all remaining variables are kept fixed.

Theorem 11.2.3   The distribution of each variable X, conditioned on the state of all other variables, is a (univariate) Gibbs distribution

$$\pi(X \mid S_x) = \frac{1}{Z_0} e^{-U(X)/T} \tag{11.6}$$

with

$$U(X) = \sum_{C \in \Theta_x} V_C(X)$$

Z_0 being a normalizing constant and C_x a set of cliques containing the variable X.

Proof. See [44, p. 281], or use the theorem of Hammersley and Clifford.

This distribution will now be used in a *Gibbs sampling* procedure. It is a kind of stochastic simulation on a Markov random field.

Definition 11.2.4 Gibbs sampling is an algorithm consisting of setting the variables of a Markov random field to arbitrary initial values, and iteratively performing the following steps for $t = 0, 1, \ldots$:

Step 1: Selecting a variable n_t according to a scheme such that:
1. For $t \to \infty$, each variable is selected infinitely often
2. There exists a $t \geq N$ such that $S \subseteq \{n_{t+1}, n_{t+2}, \ldots, n_{t+\tau}\}$ for all t

Step 2: Computing the conditional distribution for n_t by (11.6)

Step 3: Taking a sample from this distribution

Step 4: Setting the variable n_t to the value sampled

Geman and Geman [45] have discovered three useful properties of this procedure, summarized in the following three theorems.

Theorem 11.2.4 (Relaxation) Assume that for each $s \in S$, the sequence $\{n_t, \ t \geq 1\}$ contains s infinitely often. Then for every starting configuration $\omega \in \Omega$,

$$\lim_{t \to \infty} P(\mathbf{X}(t) = \omega \mid \mathbf{X}(0) = \eta) = \pi(\omega)$$

with $\mathbf{X}(t)$ being the vector of values of all variables at time t.

This theorem states that for a fixed temperature T, the sampling distribution of $\mathbf{X}(t)$ converges to posterior probability distribution π.

Theorem 11.2.5 (Annealing) Assume that there exists an integer $\tau \geq N$ such that $S \subseteq \{n_{t+1}, n_{t+2}, \ldots, n_{t+\tau}\}$ for every $t = 0, 1, 2, \ldots$. Further, let $T(t)$ be any decreasing sequence of temperatures for which

1. $T(t) \to 0$ as $t \to \infty$
2. $T(t) \geq N\Delta/\ln t$ for all $t \geq t_0$ for some integer $t_0 \geq 2$

with N the number of variables in S and Δ the maximum difference between energies for different values of a single variable.

Then for any starting configuration $\eta \in \Omega$ and for every $w \in \Omega$,

$$\lim_{t \to \infty} P(\mathbf{X}(t) = w \mid \mathbf{X}(0) = \eta) = \pi_0(w),$$

$\pi_0(w)$ being uniform distribution on

$$\Omega_0 = \{w \in \Omega : U(w) \text{ minimum of } U(\eta) \text{ over all } \eta\}.$$

This theorem provides a scheme for finding the state with the lowest energy. This scheme consists of Gibbs sampling with a *variable temperature*. The temperature must vary consistently with conditions 1 and 2.

Theorem 11.2.6 (Ergodicity)   Assume that there exists a τ such that

$$S \subseteq \{n_{t+1}, n_{t+2}, \ldots, n_{t+\tau}\}$$

for all t. Then for every function Y on Ω and for every starting configuration $\eta \in \Omega$,

$$\lim_{n \to \infty} \frac{1}{n} \sum_{t=1}^{n} Y(\mathbf{X}(t)) = \int_{\Omega} Y(w) \, d\pi(w)$$

holds with probability 1.

This theorem states that a time average of any function Y of $\mathbf{X}$ converges to the expected value of Y over π. This gives us a simple way of evaluating the expected value of any function of $\mathbf{X}$.

11.2.3   Bayesian Networks and Gibbs Sampling

After having introduced both theoretic frameworks, Bayesian networks and Gibbs sampling, we can start investigating their relationship. Their similarity, suggested by a comparison of the two graph structures and sampling algorithms, has been noted by some re-

searchers. Spiegelhalter [152] addresses the possibility of transforming the directed graph form of Bayesian networks to the indirected
graph (i.e., Markov field) form by adding edges between nodes that
are parents of the same node. This transformation is of importance
for our further reflections. Pearl sees in Markov random fields an
approach *alternative* to the stochastic simulation [122, pp. 246–247]. I
am going to show more: Stochastic simulation of Bayesian networks
can be viewed as a *special case* of Gibbs sampling.

The following theorem (Hrycej [78]) uses mapping of the directed
graph representation to the indirected graph representation as proposed by Spiegelhalter [152]. The neighborhood system in the Bayesian network is redefined so that there are edges not only to the
parents and children of a node but also to the parents of its children.
So each term $P(x_i \mid \mathbf{f}_i)$ expresses dependencies within a single clique
(see the preceding section).

Theorem 11.2.7   The variable values of a Bayesian network $\{W, C,$
$CP, E\}$ have a Gibbs distribution with regard to the neighborhood
system

$$G = C \cup \{\text{edges } e(X,Y) \text{ such that } X,Y \text{ have a common child}\}$$

with energy function

$$U(w) = -\sum_i \ln P(x_i \mid \mathbf{f}_i). \tag{11.7}$$

Proof. The joint probability of variable values w conditioned on
the evidence E is given by (11.1). Putting the energy function equal
to the negative logarithm of the joint probability and dropping the
additive constant $\ln \alpha$, we get (11.7). Each term $\ln P(x_i \mid \mathbf{f}_i)$ refers to
a clique in G, since (1) there is an edge between X_i and each node
of $\mathbf{f}_i$ in C and (2) there is an edge between any two nodes of $\mathbf{f}_i$ since
both have a common child x_i. So (11.1) corresponds to (11.3) with
$T = 1$. $\square$

An important element of sampling algorithms for both Bayesian
networks and Gibbs sampling is the univariate distribution of a single
variable. The univariate distribution of variable X of the Bayesian

network conditioned on the values of all variables from $W\backslash\{X\}$ is the concern of the following lemma.

Lemma 11.2.1 The univariate distribution of variable X of a Bayesian network $\{W, C, CP, E\}$ of Theorem 11.2.7, conditioned on the values of all variables from $W\backslash\{X\}$, is a Gibbs distribution with energy function

$$U(X) = -\ln P(X \mid \mathbf{u}_x) - \sum_j \ln P(y_j \mid \mathbf{f}_j(x)) \qquad (11.8)$$

(notation consistent with that of Section 11.2).

Proof. According to Theorem 11.2.3, the univariate distribution of each variable X conditioned on the values of all other variables is a Gibbs distribution with an energy function received by omitting all terms not containing X. Since X appears (1) in a single term $\ln P(X \mid \mathbf{u}_x)$ from (11.7) where X is a random variable conditioned on its parents $\mathbf{u}_x$ as well as (2) in some (possibly zero) number of terms $\ln P(y_j \mid \mathbf{f}_j(x))$ [received by substituting y_j for x_i and $\mathbf{f}_j(x)$ for f_i in (11.7)], where y_j is a node one of whose parents is X. So the resulting energy function is (11.8). $\qquad \square$

Theorem 11.2.8 Stochastic simulation of a Bayesian network is a special case of Gibbs sampling with energy function (11.8).

Proof. Since the equivalence of Steps 3 and 4 of both algorithms is obvious and the fixed-order selection scheme of Step 1 of the stochastic simulation algorithm satisfies the condition of Step 1 of the Gibbs sampling algorithm, it is sufficient to show that the distribution (11.2) is a special case of (11.6). But this follows immediately from Lemma 11.2.1—the energy function (11.8) is a special case of the energy function 11.6), and the Gibbs sampling with energy function (11.8) and $T = 1$ is obviously identical to a sampling from the distribution (11.2). $\qquad \square$

Theorems 11.2.7 and 11.2.8 allow an immediate formulation of statements about the convergence of stochastic sampling in Bayesian networks (see also Hrycej [78]).

Theorem 11.2.9 The distribution of each variable of a Bayesian network converges to its posterior distribution (conditioned on the given evidence).

Proof. Since, by Theorem 11.2.8, the stochastic simulation of a Bayesian network is a special case of Gibbs sampling for $T = 1$, the convergence of the distribution of each variable follows immediately from Theorem 11.2.4. ◻

Theorem 11.2.10 The time average of the value of each variable X of a Bayesian network converges to the posterior probability of x conditioned on the evidence E.

Proof. Setting $Y(X(t))$ in Theorem 11.2.6 to $X(t)$, that is, to the value of variable X in the tth iteration (with x and $\neg x$ represented by 1 and 0, respectively), we get, by Theorem 11.2.6,

$$\lim_{n \to \infty} \frac{1}{n} \sum_{t=1}^{n} X(t) = \int_{\chi} X(t) d\pi_x(x)$$
$$= P(x \mid E) \times 1 + P(\neg x \mid E) \times 0$$
$$= P(x \mid E)$$

integrating over all $x \in \chi$, that is, over both values of X, x and $\neg x$. The result is the average of X over its posterior distribution (conditioned on the evidence E), which is equal to the posterior probability of x. ◻

This theorem justifies Method A of Definition 11.2.2. It shows that the fraction of times that variable X assumes the value 1 converges to the posterior distribution of X.

Theorem 11.2.11 The time average of the distribution computed in Step 2 of the stochastic simulation algorithm converges for each variable to the posterior probability of x conditioned on the evidence E.

Proof. Let us set $Y(X(t))$ in Theorem 11.2.6 to $P(x \mid W_x(t))$, that is, to the probability of x conditioned on the set of variables $W_x =$

$W \backslash (E \cup \{X\})$. So $P(x \mid Wx(t))$ is a function of variables from W_x. By Theorem 11.2.6 we get

$$\lim_{n \to \infty} \frac{1}{n} \sum_{t=1}^{n} P(x \mid W_x(t)) = \int_{\Omega_x} P(x \mid W_x(t)) d\pi_x(\omega_x) = P(x \mid E),$$

W_x being the space of values of variables from W_x. So the convergence to the posterior probability $P(x \mid E)$ is proved. $\quad\square$

This theorem justifies Method B of Definition 11.2.2. It shows the convergence of the sampling distribution to the posterior distribution of X. Theorems 11.2.10 and 11.2.11 put on a firm basis the first type of probabilistic inference in a Bayesian network: computing posterior probabilities of nonclamped variables.

The final theorem of this section provides an algorithm for another inference type: *finding the most likely instantiation of a Bayesian network*. The most likely instantiation is the global configuration of values of logical variables that has the highest joint probability. In other words, it is *the most probable explanation of available evidence*.

Theorem 11.2.12 Suppose that stochastic sampling is performed on the distribution

$$Q(x) = \sqrt[T]{P(x \mid \mathbf{w}_x)} = \sqrt[T]{\alpha P(x \mid \mathbf{u}_x) \prod_{j} P[y_j \mid \mathbf{f}_j(x)]} \qquad (11.9)$$

T varying with t according to a schedule consistent with the conditions of Theorem 11.2.5 instead of the distribution (11.2). Then the network converges to its most likely state with probability 1.

Proof. According to Theorem 11.2.5, the annealing procedure guarantees convergence to the minimum of $U(w)$. Theorem 11.2.7 and Lemma 11.2.1 show that the joint distribution of all free variables of a Bayesian network is a Gibbs distribution with energy function (11.7), the univariate distribution of each variable being (11.8). Gibbs distribution with an energy function from (11.8) and a (variable) temperature T is obviously equal to the distribution $Q(X)$ from (11.9). Sampling from this distribution with temperature T

varying according to the annealing schedule of Theorem 11.2.5 guarantees convergence to the minimum of energy function (11.7). But the minimum of (11.7) is simultaneously the maximum of (11.1), which represents the most likely state of the variable vector w. □

The most straightforward application of this theorem is to perform the stochastic simulation of the network according to the annealing scheme and to take the final state of the network directly for the result. The number of iterations has to be sufficiently large to guarantee that the probability of reaching the most likely instantiation is sufficiently close to 1. However, it is much more efficient to proceed analogically to the algorithm of Pearl (see Section 2), that is, to compute the joint posterior probability in each iteration and to keep the record of the most likely instantiation generated so far. Modification of the algorithm of Pearl then consists merely of substituting the sampling distribution (11.9) for (11.2).

Computational experiments (Hrycej [78]) have shown the superiority of the annealing algorithm over the constant-temperature relaxation algorithm used so far (Pearl [123]). On a Bayesian network with 20 nonclamped and six clamped nodes, the constant-temperature algorithm of Pearl and the variable-temperature annealing algorithm of Theorem 11.2.5 have been tested. The results are presented in Table 11.1. Theorem 11.2.5 would prescribe starting temperatures higher than 1, but would then take an unacceptably long time to reach the low temperatures that are so important for finding the maximum. The scheme seems to perform well even with substantially lower starting temperatures. The same experience has been reported by Geman and Geman [45]. They suggest that the lower

TABLE 11.1 Computational Experience with Annealing Scheme

Starting temperature	1.00	1.00
Temperature after 50 iterations	1.00	0.18
After 10 iterations	0.1761	0.4403
After 20 iterations	0.1761	0.7925
After 30 iterations	0.1761	0.7925
After 40 iterations	0.1761	0.7925
After 50 iterations	0.2752	0.7925

bound of Theorem 11.2.5 for the starting temperature is excessively pessimistic.

11.2.4 Bayesian Networks and the Boltzmann Machine

Let us briefly summarize our discussion in the previous sections. An artificial intelligence model, Bayesian networks, with a clear symbolic interpretation, and a general framework for stochastic sampling on Markov random fields, also applicable to stochastic neural networks, have been presented. The isomorphy of the two models has been shown for both the representation and inference algorithms. We can now use this knowledge for the primary goal of this chapter: finding an interpretation of (possibly prestructured) neural networks in terms of probabilistic relationships between the symbolic statements assigned to neural network nodes.

Although some simple *feedforward models* (based on principles different from those of Gibbs sampling) have been assigned an explicit probabilistic interpretation (see, e.g., Kohonen [91, pp. 187–188]), this has not been the case for *relaxation-based neural network models*. Probably the best known of them is the *Boltzmann machine*, described, for example, by Hinton and Sejnowski [64].

Note 11.2.3 The analysis of this section is closely related to that of Geffner and Pearl [43] for another connectionist model, the Hopfield network, which is a deterministic variant of the Boltzmann machine.

Definition 11.2.5 The **Boltzmann machine** is a graph $\{SB, GB\}$, whose nodes are activated or inactivated (i.e., assigned values 1 or 0, respectively) according to the following scheme:

1. The input of each node X_l is given by the weighted sum of the activations of all its neighbors X_j decreased by the threshold θ_i:

$$Inp_{X_i} = \sum_j wjiX_j - \theta_i. \tag{11.10}$$

2. The probability of activation of X_i is

$$PA_{X_i} = \frac{1}{1 + e^{-Inp_{x_i}/T}}. \tag{11.11}$$

The weights are assumed to be symmetric: $w_{ij} = w_{ji}$.

A general Bayesian network obviously cannot be viewed as a Boltzmann machine since the activation of each variable cannot be expressed as a function of a weighted sum of activations of its neighbor variables. So we have to find additional assumptions that would simplify the form of the probability distribution. One such assumption is that of the *mutual independence* of parent variables. As shown by Shastri and Feldman [145], it is formally equivalent to the *maximal entropy* assumption. This assumption is used frequently if the complete set of conditional probabilities of the form $P(x \mid \mathbf{u}_x)$ is not available. The following theorem (Hrycej [80]) states that under this assumption, a Bayesian network is equivalent to a Boltzmann machine.

Note 11.2.4   The assumption of conditional and unconditional dependence is too strong to be of practical importance if taken rigorously. However, it is a widely used approximation if further information is unavailable (see, e.g., Kim and Pearl [90]).

Theorem 11.2.13   If the parent variables U_i of each variable X of a Bayesian network are independent of X both unconditionally and conditionally, the Bayesian network is equivalent to a Boltzmann machine.

Proof. By the Bayes rule, the conditional probability $P(x \mid \&u_i)$ [with u_i representing parents of x and $P(x)$ the prior probability of x] can be written as

$$P(x \mid \&_i u_i) = \frac{P(\&_i u_i \mid x)P(x)}{P(\&_i u_i)}. \qquad (11.12)$$

Assuming conditional and unconditional independence of the parents of x,

$$P(\&_i u_i \mid x) = \prod_i P(u_i \mid x)$$

and

$$P(\&_i u_i) = \prod_i P(u_i),$$

(11.12) can be written as

$$P(x \mid \&_i u_i) = P(x)^{1-n} \prod_i P(x \mid u_i)$$

with n the number of parents. (Note that this relation is formally analogous to the best estimate rule of Shastri and Feldman [145] for evidential reasoning.)

Since the probabilities $P(y_j \mid f_j(x))$ are now expressed as a product of probabilities one of which contains x, (11.2) becomes

$$P(x \mid \mathbf{w}_x) = \alpha P(x)^{1-n} \prod_i P(x \mid u_i) \prod_j P(y_j \mid x). \qquad (11.13)$$

If we define the ratio $PR_x = P(x \mid \mathbf{w}_x)/P(\neg x \mid \mathbf{w}_x)$, the sampling probabilities of x and $\neg x$ become $PR_x/(1 + PR_x)$ and $1/(1 + PR_x)$, respectively. According to (11.13), PR_x can be written as

$$PR_x = \left(\frac{P(x)}{P(\neg x)} \right)^{1-n}. \qquad (11.14)$$

Let us introduce the functions $R_x(U_i)$ and $S_x(Y_j)$ of variables U_i and Y_j such that

$$
\begin{aligned}
R_x(u_i) &= \ln P(x \mid u_i) - \ln P(\neg x \mid u_i) = A_{xu_i} \\
R_x(\neg u_i) &= \ln P(x \mid \neg u_i) - \ln P(\neg x \mid \neg u_i) = B_{xu_i} \\
S_x(y_j) &= \ln P(y_j \mid x) - \ln P(y_j \mid \neg x) = C_{xy_j} \\
S_x(\neg y_j) &= \ln P(\neg y_j \mid x) - \ln P(\neg y_j \mid \neg x) = D_{xy_j}.
\end{aligned}
\qquad (11.15)
$$

If we represent u_i and $\neg u_i$ (or y_j and $\neg y_j$) by the numerical values 1 and 0, respectively, linear functions satisfying the conditions of (11.15) are

$$R_x(U_i) = (A_{xu_i} - B_{xu_i})U_i + B_{xu_i}$$

and

$$S_x(Y_j) = (C_{xy_j} - D_{xy_j})Y_j + D_{xy_j}.$$

The logarithm of (11.14) can be written as

$$\ln PR_x = \sum_i (A_{xu_i} - B_{xu_i})U_i + \sum_j (C_{xy_j} - D_{xy_j})Y_j - \theta_x \qquad (11.16)$$

with

$$\theta_x = (n-1)E_x - \sum_i B_{xu_i} - \sum_j D_{xy_j}$$

and

$$E_x = \ln P(x) - \ln P(\neg x).$$

Formula (11.16) is obviously equivalent to the input function of a Boltzmann machine according to (11.10); with weights $A_{xy} - B_{xy} = C_{yx} - D_{yx}$, the weights are symmetric. The equivalence of the activation function (11.11) can be seen from the probability of activation of x, with $Inp_x = \ln PR_x$ and $T = 1$:

$$\frac{PR_x}{1 + PR_x} = \frac{1}{1 + 1/PR_x} = \frac{1}{1 + e^{-\ln PR_x}}.$$

So the equivalence to the Boltzmann machine is proved.   □

The theorem shows that given a set of N unconditional probabilities $P(x)$ and M positive conditional probabilities $P(x \mid y)$, N thresholds and M weights of a Boltzmann machine with N nodes and M edges can be computed. This is always possible since conditional probabilities

$$P(x \mid \neg y) = \frac{P(x) - P(x \mid y)P(y)}{1 - P(y)}$$

result directly from $P(x)$, $P(y)$, and $P(x \mid y)$.

To get a *probabilistic interpretation of a Boltzmann machine* with given weights and nodes, M weights and N nodes provide $M + N$ equations for $M + N$ variables (conditional and unconditional probabilities). To get a unique equation set, edges must be assigned a direction such that the graph is noncyclic. Since the equations are cubic, the existence of a unique solution for any set of weights and thresholds is not guaranteed.

The correspondence between weights and probabilities may become more direct under further simplifying assumptions. For example, the assumption of $P(x) = P(\neg x) = 0.5$ for all variables implies that

$$P(\neg x \mid \neg y) = P(x \mid y)$$

and

$$P(\neg x \mid y) = P(x \mid \neg y) = 1 - P(x \mid y).$$

The weights and thresholds of (11.16) can then be simplified to

$$w_{xy} = 2(\ln P(x \mid y) - \ln(1 - P(x \mid y))) = 2R_{xy}$$

$$\theta_x = -\sum_y R_{xy}. \qquad (11.17)$$

Obviously, the probabilistic interpretation of every Boltzmann machine satisfying the condition

$$\theta_x = -0.5 \sum_y w_{xy}$$

for each x can easily be found using (11.17).

If the set of admissible variable values is modified from $\{0,1\}$ to $\{-1,1\}$, the conditions for weights and thresholds characterizing this class of Boltzmann machines become even simpler:

$$w_{xy} = R_{xy}$$

$$\theta_x = 0.$$

So each Boltzmann machine with zero weights and value set $\{-1,1\}$ can be interpreted as a Bayesian network with:

1. Independent conditional and unconditional probabilities
2. Unconditional probabilities of each variable equal to 0.5

3. Conditional probabilities

$$P(x \mid y) = P(y \mid x) = \frac{e^{w_{xy}}}{1 - e^{w_{xy}}}.$$

Note 11.2.5 Although the assumption of all unconditional probabilities being 0.5 may seem unrealistic for systems with variables representing artificial concepts, it may be more realistic for lower-level systems such as those for pattern recognition. The advantage of such balanced variables is in its *high information content*—a two-valued stochastic variable with probabilities of both states equal to 0.5 has the maximal entropy. Such an optimal (or nearly optimal) coding is exactly the advantage of distributed representations in some connectionist models (see [66]). So balanced (or nearly balanced) variables of this type may frequently occur in biological, or biologically oriented, systems.

11.3 SUPPORTING LEARNING BY USING EXPLICIT KNOWLEDGE

An important result of Section 11.2 is that there is a direct relationship between a Boltzmann machine on the neural network side and a Bayesian network on the knowledge representation side. With this relationship in mind, a procedure combining knowledge-based design of network topology and determining network parameters by learning from examples can be proposed. It consists of the following steps:

1. *Network Construction*
   (a) The application domain concepts relevant for the given task are collected and formulated in a set of propositional variables. Each of these propositional variables becomes a network node.
   (b) Causal relations between propositions are formulated. The existence of a causal relation between two nodes is represented by a directed edge. The result of this step is a sparsely connected nonlayered network.
2. *Weight Initialization.* There are three classes of weights, differing in the degree to which they can be determined by explicit

knowledge:

(a) Conditional probabilities that are known with sufficient accuracy are used to determine fixed weights by Theorem 11.2.13.

(b) Probabilities for which reasonable estimates are available are used to assess good initial values for certain weights.

(c) Remaining weights are set to random initial weights.

3. *Learning by Example.* A learning procedure such as the one of Ackley et al. [3] is used to infer optimal weights.

11.4 RELATED WORK

Geman [44] proposed a very general approach to probabilistic reasoning based on Gibbs sampling. His approach consists of:

1. Formulating an arbitrary (consistent) set of probabilistic constraints, such as conditional or marginal probabilities, in the form

$$E[F_a(\mathbf{x})] = 0, \qquad a \in A$$

with A a set of indices of all probabilistic constraints.

2. Looking for the prior joint probability distribution $\pi(\mathbf{x})$ satisfying these constraints that has a maximum entropy. This amounts to maximizing the expression

$$H = -\sum \pi(\mathbf{x}) \ln \pi(\mathbf{x}),$$

which can be found in the Gibbs form

$$\pi(\mathbf{x}) = \frac{1}{Z} e^{\sum_{a \in A} \lambda_a F_a(\mathbf{x})}, \qquad \mathbf{x} \in \Omega$$

with λ_a representing Lagrange multipliers and Z a normalizing constant.

3. Generating the posterior distribution (conditioned on the available evidence) by Gibbs sampling.

The maximum-entropy constraint ensures completeness in under-constrained cases (see also the analytical approaches of Cheeseman [25] and Shastri and Feldman [145]).

The price for the generality of this approach is the necessity of determining the Lagrange multipliers for prior distribution. Geman suggests a gradient method based on stochastic relaxation. This method can be viewed as a learning method for a certain type of connectionist network (and is, in fact, related to the gradient learning method of Ackley et al. [3] for a special type of Gibbs sampling model, the Boltzmann machine). However, this method requires a complete stochastic–relaxation (i.e., Gibbs sampling) cycle for *each* gradient step and is thus computationally expensive. Another problem is posed by the consistency assumption, which may be difficult to verify for arbitrary probabilistic constraints.

The Bayesian network approach imposes some restrictions on the probabilistic constraints:

- The constraints are of the form $P(x \mid \mathbf{u}_x)$, with x a single variable.
- There must be an indexing of the variables that constitutes a partial order; that is, the Bayesian network has to be acyclic.
- The conditional probability distributions must be specified completely; that is, the conditional probabilities for each variable conditioned on all value combinations of all parents must be known.

The first two constraints provide the consistency (see the Note 11.2.1). According to Pearl and Verma [124], the expressiveness of the model can be extended by introducing auxiliary variables and is probably sufficient for most practical tasks (the expressiveness of various models is discussed in [123, Sec. 3.3.3]). The last constraint may have a more serious impact on practical applications. However, some methods of estimation of missing parameters have been suggested, for example, by Kim and Pearl [90].

The reward for these constraints is the computational simplicity of this approach. The prior Gibbs distribution is specified completely by the conditional probabilities, so that no learning phase, corresponding to the determination of Lagrange multipliers, is necessary. Moreover, the sampling probabilities (11.2) happen to be directly equal to the product of conditional probabilities containing the variable sampled.

In the area of the relationship between Bayesian and connectionist networks, there are several investigations closely related to the one presented here. Geffner and Pearl [43] have studied the probabilistic interpretation of the Hopfield network. They showed that each weight w_{xy} of a Hopfield network between nodes X and Y can be interpreted as

$$w_{xy} = \ln P(x \mid y) - \ln P(\neg x \mid y) - \ln P(x \mid \neg y) + \ln P(\neg x \mid \neg y).$$

So the Hopfield network is capable of capturing second-order probabilistic constraints. Higher-order constraints can be captured by a network analogous to the Hopfield network, with a multiplicative rather than an additive activation rule. However, since the activation function of the Hopfield network is deterministic, Gibbs sampling theorems cannot be applied to it. Consequently, a Bayesian network transformed into a Hopfield network would not converge to the globally most probable state, nor would the frequencies of activation of individual nodes converge to the posterior probabilities.

A similar interpretation of the weights of another connectionist model, the Boltzmann machine, has been put forth by Hinton and Sejnowski [65]. Unlike the Hopfield network, the Boltzmann machine has a stochastic rather than a deterministic activation rule (see Hinton and Sejnowski [64]). So it is a direct instance of the Gibbs sampling procedure and can be interpreted as a Bayesian network for second-order probabilistic constraints.

CHAPTER 12 ———————————

Conclusions

What remains to be done is to summarize what we have learned about the potential of modularization of neural network learning. The theoretical analyses and computational experiments of this book provide evidence supporting the following general conclusions:

1. Modularization of neural network learning (in the sense used throughout the book) is an appropriate means of improving learning performance in both convergence and generalization.
2. Most modularization approaches allow an explicit decomposition of the learning task into development stages with partial success criteria for each.

The individual approaches to modularization investigated in this book have the following properties:

- *Supporting supervised learning by feature discovery* improves the learning performance for classification problems with the following characteristics:
  1. They are not very nonlinear (i.e., linear classifiers perform satisfactorily on them).
  2. There are substantial dependencies between input variables (i.e., there is a potential for compression into a rel-

atively small number of features). This is almost always the case if the number of input variables is high.

- *Supporting supervised learning by quantization* has a very broad application potential. It is applicable even to problems for which linear classifiers do not perform well. Both algorithms used, the one-dimensional quantization algorithm and loss function–based perceptron learning, have the advantage of guaranteed convergence to desired optimal states. Since the supervised learning procedure is linear, there is no problem of overlearning. Linear separating hyperplanes have zero derivatives of order higher that 1 and are thus optimally smooth in the sense of regularization theory.

- *Supervised feature discovery* is a logical continuation of unsupervised feature discovery. However, its superiority over unsupervised feature discovery could not be confirmed by computational experiments. Since this may result from an unsatisfactory convergence, it may be worth further investigation.

- *Decomposition of the network to minimize the interactions* results in a drastic improvement in convergence reliability and robustness with regard to various learning rates. Its commitment to mean-squared error as an error measure makes it more suitable for learning continuous mappings than for classification problems. For classification problems, the use of loss function approximations improves the efficiency of learning to an extent that cannot always be traded off by the convergence improvement of layer-by-layer learning.

- *Modularization of application tasks* is certainly a technique with a high potential for making learning more efficient (perhaps by several orders of magnitude). Because of its variability, assessment of this technique is beyond the scope of this book, but I believe it will become one of the most powerful modularization approaches, in particular for nonclassifier applications such as regulation, control, and autonomous systems.

- *Decomposition of learning into a knowledge-based determination of network structure and learning of network parameters* makes sense for nonlayered, feedback networks. Since a correspondence between causal probabilistic networks and neural networks of Boltzmann machine type could be established, it is possible to construct a neural network that reflects the structural dependencies of the application domain. Optimal network weights can then be found using a learning algorithm.

References

1. Aborn, M., and Rubenstein, H., Information theory and immediate recall, *Journal of Experimental Psychology* **44** (4) (1952).
2. Abu-Mostafa, Y. S., The Vapnik–Chervonenkis dimension: information versus complexity in learning, *Neural Computation* **1** (1989): 312–317.
3. Ackley, D. H., Hinton, G. E., and Sejnowski, T. J., A learning algorithm for Boltzmann machines, *Cognitive Science* **9** (1985): 147–169.
4. Albus, J. S., A new approach to manipulator control: the cerebellar model articulation controller (CMAC), *Trans. ASME, Journal of Dynamic Systems, Measurement and Control* **97** (1975): 220–227.
5. Albus, J. S., *Brain, Behavior, and Robotics*, BYTE Books, 1981.
6. Allen, G. I., and Tsukahara, N., Cerebrocerebellar communication systems, *Physiological Review* **54** (1974): 957–1006.
7. Anderberg, M. R., *Cluster Analysis for Applications*, Academic Press, New York, 1973.
8. Anshelevich, V. V., et al., On the ability of neural networks to perform generalization by induction, *Biological Cybernetics* **61** (1989): 125–128.
9. Baldi, P., and Meir, R., Computing with arrays of coupled oscillators: an application to preattentive texture discrimination, *Neural Computation* **2** (1990): 458–471.
10. Ballard, D. H., Modular learning in neural networks, in: *Proc. National Conference on Artificial Intelligence*, Seattle, WA, 1987, pp. 279–284.

11. Barlow, H. B., Unsupervised learning, *Neural Computation* **1** (1989): 295–311.

12. Barto, A. G., Sutton, R. S., and Anderson, C. W., Neuronlike adaptive elements that can solve difficult learning control problems, *IEEE Transactions on Systems, Man and Cybernetics* **SMC-13** (5) (1983).

13. Baum, E. G., The perceptron algorithm is fast for nonmalicious distributions, *Neural Computation* **2** (1990): 249–260.

14. Baum, E. G., A polynomial time algorithm that learns two hidden unit nets, *Neural Computation* **2** (1990): 510–522.

15. Baum, E. G., and Haussler, D., What size net gives valid generalization? *Neural Computation* **1** (1989): 151–160.

16. Beer, R. D., *Intelligence as Adaptive Behavior*, Academic Press, New York, 1990.

17. Besag, J., Spatial interaction and the statistical analysis of lattice systems (with discussion), *Journal of the Royal Statistical Society, Series B* **36** (1974): 192–326.

18. Bourlard, H., and Kamp, Y., Auto-association by multilayer perceptrons and singular value decomposition, *Biological Cybernetics* **59** (1988): 291–294.

19. Breiman, L., Friedman, J., Olshen, R., and Stone, C., *Classification and Regression Trees*, Wadsworth, Belmont, CA, 1984.

20. Brooks, R. A., A robot that walks: emergent behaviors from a carefully evolved network, *Neural Computation* **1** (1989): 253–262.

21. Cajal, S. R., *Histologie du système de l'homme et des vertébrés*, Maloine, Paris, 1911.

22. Carpenter, G., and Grossberg, S., Neural dynamics of category learning and recognition: attention, memory consolidation, and amnesia, in: Davis, J., Newburgh, R., and Wegman, E. (Eds.), *Brain Structure, Learning and Memory*, AAAS Symposium Series, 1986.

23. Carpenter, G., and Grossberg, S., A massively parallel architecture for a self-organizing neural pattern recognition machine, *Computer Vision, Graphics, and Image Processing* **37** (1987): 54–115.

24. Carpenter, G., and Grossberg, S., ART 2: Self-organization of stable category recognition codes for analog input patterns, *Applied Optics* **26(23)** (1987): 4919–4930.

25. Cheeseman, P., A method of computing generalized Bayesian probability values for expert systems, in: *Proc. 8th International Joint Conference on Artificial Intelligence*, Karlsruhe, Germany, 1983, pp. 198–202.

26. Devijver, P. A., and Kittler, J., *Pattern Recognition: A Statistical Approach*, Prentice Hall, Englewood Cliffs, NJ, 1982.

27. Duda, R. O., and Hart, P. E., *Pattern Classification and Scene Analysis*, Wiley, New York, 1973.

28. Dvoretzky, A., On stochastic approximation, in: *Proc. 3rd Berkeley Symposium on Mathematical Statistics and Probability*, Vol. 1, Berkeley, CA, 1956, pp. 39–55.

29. Eccles, J. C., *The Understanding of the Brain*, McGraw-Hill, New York, 1973.

30. Eccles, J. C., Ito, M., and Szentágothai, J., *The Cerebellum as a Neuronal Machine*, Springer-Verlag, Berlin, 1967.

31. Eckmiller, R., Neural nets for sensory and motor trajectories, *IEEE Control Systems Magazine* **9** (1989): 53–59.

32. Eckmiller, R., Pulse processing neural systems for motor control, in: *Proc. International Conference on Artificial Neural Networks*, Espoo, Finland, 1991, pp. 345–350.

33. Erwin, E., Obermayer, K., and Schulten, K., Convergence properties of self-organizing maps, in: *Proc. International Conference on Artificial Neural Networks*, Espoo, Finland, 1991, pp. 409–414.

34. Evarts, E. V., Representation of movements and muscles by pyramidal tract neurons of the precentral motor cortex, in: Yahr, M. D., and Purpura, D. F. (Eds.), *Neurophysiological Basis of Normal and Abnormal Motor Activity*, Raven Press, New York, 1967.

35. Fahlman, S. E., An empirical study of learning speed, *Technical Report CMU-CS-88-162*, Carnegie-Mellon University, Pittsburgh, PA, 1988.

36. Fisher, R., The use of multiple measurements in taxonomic problems, *Annals of Eugenics* **7** (1936): 179–188.

37. Frank, H., *Kybernetische Grundlagen der Pädagogik*, Agis-Verlag, Baden-Baden, Germany, 1962.

38. Frank, H., Über die Kapazitäten menschlicher Sinnesorgane, *Grundlagenstudien aus Kybernetik und Geisteswissenschaft* **I** (5) (1960): 145–152.

39. Fu, K. S., *Sequential Methods in Pattern Recognition and Machine Learning*, Academic Press, New York, 1968.

40. Fukunaga, K., and Koontz, W. L. G., Application of the Karhunen–Loewe expansion to feature selection and ordering, *IEEE Transactions on Computers* **C-19** (1) (1974): 28–33.

41. Fukushima, K. S., Miyake, S., and Ito, T., Neocognitron: a neural network model for a mechanism of visual pattern recognition, *IEEE Transactions on Systems, Man and Cybernetics* **SMC-13** (1983): 826–834.

42. Gallant S. I., A connectionist learning algorithm with provable generalization and scaling bounds, *Neural Networks* **3** (1990): 191–201.

43. Geffner, H., and Pearl, J., On the probabilistic semantics of connectionist networks, in: *Proc. First IEEE International Conference on Neural Networks*, San Diego, CA, 1987, pp. 187–195.

44. Geman, S., Stochastic relaxation methods for image restoration and expert systems, in: Cooper, D. B., et al. (Eds.), *Automated Image Analysis: Theory and Experiments*, Academic Press, New York, 1985; also in: Erickson, G. J., and Smith, C. R. (Eds.), *Maximum-Entropy and Bayesian Methods in Science and Engineering*, Vol. 2, Kluwer Academic Publishers, Hingham, MA, 1988, pp. 265–311.

45. Geman, S., and Geman, D., Stochastic relaxation, Gibbs distributions and the Bayesian restoration of images, *IEEE Transactions on Pattern Analysis and Machine Intelligence* **6** (6) (1984): 721–742.

46. Giles, C. L., and Maxwell, T., Learning, invariance, and generalization in high-order neural networks, *Applied Optics* **26** (23) (1987): 4972–4978.

47. Graham, D. P. W., and D'Eleuterio, G. M. T., Robotic control using a modular architecture of cooperative artificial neural networks, in: *Proc. International Conference on Artificial Neural Networks*, Espoo, Finland, 1991, pp. 365–370.

48. Grossberg, S., *Studies in Mind and Brain*, D. Reidel, Dordrecht, The Netherlands, 1982.

49. Grossberg, S., On the development of feature detectors in the visual cortex with applications to learning and reaction–diffusion systems, *Biological Cybernetics* **21** (1976): 145–159.

50. Grossberg, S., Adaptive pattern classification and universal recoding I: Parallel development and coding of neural feature detectors, *Biological Cybernetics* **23** (1976): 121–134.

51. Grossberg, S., Competitive learning: from interactive activation to adaptive resonance, *Cognitive Science* **11** (1987): 23–63.

52. Grossberg, S. (Ed.), *The Adaptive Brain*, North-Holland, Amsterdam, 1987.

53. Grossberg, S., and Kuperstein, M., *Neural Dynamics of Adaptive Sensory-Motor Control*, North-Holland, Amsterdam, 1986.

54. Ji, C., Snapp, R. R., and Psaltis, D., Generalizing smoothness constraints from discrete samples, *Neural Computation* **2** (1990): 188–197.

55. Hartigan, J. A., *Clustering Algorithms*, Wiley, New York, 1975.

56. Haussler, D., Generalizing the PAC model for neural nets and other learning applications, *Report UCSC-CLR-8930*, University of California, Santa Cruz, September 1989.

57. Hampson, S. E., and Volper, D. J., Linear function neurons: structure and training, *Biological Cybernetics* **53** (1986): 203–217.

58. Hampson, S. E., and Volper, D. J., Disjunctive models of Boolean category learning, *Biological Cybernetics* **56** (1987): 121–137.

59. Hand, D. J., *Discrimination and Classification*, Wiley, Chichester, West Sussex, England, 1981.

60. Harris, R. W., and Ledwidge, T. J., *Introduction to Noise Analysis*, Pion, London, 1974.

61. Hebb, D. O., *The Organization of Behavior*, Wiley, New York, 1949.

62. Hecht-Nielsen, R., Counterpropagation networks, *Applied Optics*, **26** (23) (1987): 4979–4984.

63. Hertz, J., Krogh, A., and Palmer, R. G., *Introduction to the Theory of Neural Computation*, Addison-Wesley, Reading, MA, 1991.

64. Hinton, G. E., and Sejnowski, T. J., Learning and relearning in Boltzmann machines, in: Rumelhart, D. E., and McClelland, J. L., et al. (Eds.), *Parallel Distributed Processing—Explorations in the Microstructure of Cognition*, MIT Press, Cambridge, MA, 1986, pp. 282–317.

65. Hinton, G. E., and Sejnowski, T. J., Optimal perceptual inference, in: *Proc. IEEE Computer Society Conference on Computer Vision and Pattern Recognition*, Washington, DC, 1983.

66. Hinton, G. E., McClelland, J. L., and Rumelhart, D. E., Distributed representations, in: Rumelhart, D. E., and McClelland, J. L., et al. (Eds.), *Parallel Distributed Processing—Explorations in the Microstructure of Cognition*, MIT Press, Cambridge, MA, 1986, pp. 77–109.

67. Ho, C., On multi-layered connectionist models: adding layers vs. increasing width, in: *Proc. 11th International Joint Conference on Artificial Intelligence*, Vol. 1, Detroit, MI, 1988, pp. 176–179.

68. Hocking, R. R., Developments in linear regression methodology: 1952–1982, *Technometrics* **25** (1983): 219–249.

69. Hopfield, J. J., Neural networks and physical systems with emergent collective computational abilities, *Proc. National Academy of Science* **79** (1982): 2554–2558.

70. Hopfield, J. J., and Tank, D. W., Neural computation of decisions in optimization problems, *Biological Cybernetics* **52** (1985): 141–152.

71. Howes, D. H., and Solomon, R. L., Visual duration threshold as a duration of word-probability, *Journal of Experimental Psychology* **41** (6) (1951).

72. Hrycej, T., Unsupervised learning by backward inhibition, in: *Proc. 11th International Joint Conference on Artificial Intelligence*, Detroit, MI, 1989, pp. 170–175.

73. Hrycej, T., Backward inhibition: a mechanism for unsupervised discovery of input features, *Journal of Cognitive Systems* **2–3** (June 1989): 233–250.

74. Hrycej, T., A non-competitive model for unsupervised learning, in: *Proc. First IEE International Conference on Artificial Neural Networks*, London, 1989, pp. 233–237.

75. Hrycej, T., Self-organization by delta rule, in: *Proc. International Joint Conference on Neural Networks*, Vol. II, San Diego, CA, 1990, pp. 307–312.

76. Hrycej, T., Supporting supervised learning by self-organization, *Neurocomputing* **3** (1991/92).

77. Hrycej, T., A modular architecture for efficient learning, in: *Proc. International Joint Conference on Neural Networks*, Vol. I, San Diego, CA, 1990, pp. 557–562.

78. Hrycej, T., Gibbs sampling in Bayesian networks, *Artificial Intelligence* **46** (1990).

79. Hrycej, T., On the relationship between information processing in probabilistic and neural networks, in: *Proc. International Conference on Fuzzy Logic and Neural Networks*, Iizuka, Japan, 1990.

80. Hrycej, T., Common features of neural-network models of high and low level human information processing, in: *Proc. International Conference on Artificial Neural Networks*, Espoo, Finland, 1991, pp. 861–866.

81. Hrycej, T., Neural classifiers using loss functions, *International Joint Conference on Neural Networks*, Seattle, WA, 1991.

82. Hrycej, T., Misclassification loss in neural network classifiers, submitted to *Neural Networks*.

83. Hrycej, T., Back to single-layer learning principles, *International Joint Conference on Neural Networks*, Seattle, WA, 1991.

84. Judd, S., The complexity of learning in constrained neural networks, in: *Proc. Conference on Neural Information Processing Systems—Natural and Synthetic*, IEEE, 1987.

85. Kacmarz, S., Angenäherte Auflösung von Systemen linearer Gleichungen, *Bulletin International de l'Academie Polonaise des Sciences et des Letters, Classe Sciences Mathematiques* (1937).

86. Katz, A. J., Gately, M. T., and Collins, D. R., Robust classifiers without robust features, *Neural Computation* **2** (1990): 472–479.

87. Kämmerer, B. R., Improving generalization properties by use of the uncertainty network, in: *Proc. International Conference on Artificial Neural Networks*, Espoo, Finland, 1991, pp. 855–860.

88. Kämmerer, B. R., and Küpper, W. A., Design of hierarchical perceptron structures and their application to the task of isolated-word recognition, in: *Proc. International Joint Conference on Neural Networks*, Washington, DC, 1989, pp. 243–249.

89. Kiefer, J., and Wolfowitz, J., Stochastic estimation of the maximum of a regression function, *Annals of Mathematical Statistics* **23** (1952): 462–466.

90. Kim, J. H., and Pearl, J., A computational model for causal and diagnostic reasoning in inference systems, in: *Proc. 8th International Joint Conference on Artificial Intelligence*, Karlsruhe, 1983, pp. 190–193.

91. Kohonen, T., *Self-Organization and Associative Memory*, Springer-Verlag, New York, 1984.

92. Kohonen, T., Barna, G., and Chrisley, R., Statistical pattern recognition with neural networks: benchmarking studies, in: *Proc. IEEE International Conference on Neural Networks*, San Diego, CA, 1988, pp. 61–67.

93. Kosko, B., Bidirectional associative memories, *IEEE Transactions on Systems, Man and Cybernetics* **SMC-18** (1987): 49–60.

94. Kreßel, U., The impact of the learning-set size in handwritten-digit recognition, in: *Proc. International Conference on Artificial Neural Networks*, Espoo, Finland, 1991.

95. Kreßel, U., Franke, J., and Schürmann, J., Polynomklassifikator versus Multilayer-Perzeptron, *12th DAGM-Symposium*, 1990.

96. Kung, S. Y., and Hwang, J. N., An algebraic projection analysis for optimal hidden units size and learning rates in back-propagation, in: *Proc. IEEE International Conference on Neural Networks*, San Diego, CA, 1988, pp. 363–370.

97. Leen, T., Rudnick, M., and Hammerstrom, D., Hebbian feature discovery improves classifier efficiency, in: *Proc. International Joint Conference on Neural Networks*, Vol. I, San Diego, CA, 1990, pp. 51–56.

98. Lebowitz, M., Classifying numerical information for generalization, *Cognitive Science* **9** (1985).

99. LeCun, Y., et al., Backpropagation applied to handwritten zip code recognition, *Neural Computation* **1** (1989): 541–551.

100. Lefebvre, T., Nicolas, J. M., and Degoul, P., Numerical to symbolical conversion for acoustic signal classification using a two-stage neural architecture, in: *Proc. International Neural Network Conference*, Paris, 1990, pp. 119–122.

101. Linden, A., and Kindermann, J., Inversion of multi-layer nets, in: *Proc. International Joint Conference on Neural Networks*, Washington, DC, 1989.

102. Lippmann, R. P., An introduction to computing with neural nets, *Computer Architecture News* **16** (1) (1988): 7–25.

103. Linsker, R., Self-organization in a perceptual network, *Computer* (March 1988): 105–117.

104. MacKay, D. M., and McCulloch, W. L., The limiting information capacity of a neuronal link, *Bulletin of Mathematical Biophysics* **14** (1952).

105. Malsburg, C. von der, Self-organization of orientation sensitive cells in the striate cortex, *Kybernetik* **14** (1973): 85–100.

106. Martinetz, T., and Schulten, K., A "neural-gas" network learns topologies, in: *Proc. International Conference on Artificial Neural Networks*, Espoo, Finland, 1991, pp. 397–402.

107. McCulloch, W. S., and Pitts, W., A logical calculus of the ideas immanent in nervous activity, *Bulletin of Mathematical Biophysics* **5** (1943): 115–133.

108. Miller, G. A., Brunner, J. S., and Postman, L., Familiarity of letter sequences and tachistoscopic identification, *Journal of Genetic Psychology* **50** (1954): 129–139.

109. Miller, W. T., Granz, F. H., and Kraft, L. G., Application of a general learning algorithm to the control of robotic manipulators, *International Journal of Robotics* **6** (1987): 84–98.

110. Minsky, M., and Papert, S., *The Perceptrons*, MIT Press, Cambridge, MA, 1968.

111. Munro, P., A dual backpropagation scheme for scalar reward learning, *Proc. 9th Annual Conference of Cognitive Science Society*, 1987, pp. 165–176.

112. Narendra, K. S., and Thathachar, M. A. L., *Learning Automata: An Introduction*, Prentice Hall, Englewood Cliffs, NJ, 1989.

113. Nguyen, D., and Widrow, B., The truck backer-upper: an example of self-learning in neural networks, in: *Proc. International Joint Conference on Neural Networks*, Vol. 2, Washington, DC, 1989, pp. 357–363.

114. Oja, E., A simplified neuron model as a principal component analyzer, *Journal of Mathematical Biology* **15** (1982): 267–273.

115. Oja, E., Neural networks, principal components, and subspaces, *International Journal of Neural Systems* **1** (1) (1989): 61–68.

116. Oja, E., and Kohonen, T., The subspace learning algorithm as a formalism for pattern recognition and neural networks, in: *Proc. IEEE International Conference on Neural Networks*, San Diego, CA, 1988, pp. 277–284.

117. Orfanidis, S. J., Gram–Schmidt neural nets, *Neural Computation* **2** (1990): 116–126.

118. Pao, Y.-H., *Adaptive Pattern Recognition and Neural Networks*, Addison-Wesley, Reading, MA, 1989.

119. Pearl, J., On evidential reasoning in a hierarchy of hypotheses, *Artificial Intelligence* **28** (1986): 9–15.

120. Pearl, J., Fusion, propagation and structuring in belief networks, *Artificial Intelligence* **29** (1986): 241–288.

121. Pearl, J., A constraint-propagation approach to probabilistic reasoning, in: Kanal, L. N., and Lemmer, J. F. (Eds.), *Uncertainty in Artificial Intelligence*, North-Holland, Amsterdam, 1986, pp. 357–369.

122. Pearl, J., Evidential reasoning using stochastic simulation of causal models, *Artificial Intelligence* **32** (1987): 245–257.

123. Pearl, J., *Probabilistic Reasoning in Intelligent Systems*, Morgan Kaufmann, London, 1988.

124. Pearl, J., and Verma, T., The logic of representing dependencies by directed graphs, in: *Proc. 6th National Conference on Artificial Intelligence*, Seattle, WA, 1987, pp. 374–379.

125. Piaget, J., *Meine Theorie der geistigen Intelligenz*, Fischer Taschenbuch Verlag, Frankfurt, Germany, 1983.

126. Piaget, J., *Psychologie der Intelligenz*, Klett-Cotta, Stuttgart, Germany, 1984.

127. Piaget, J., and Inhelder, B., *Die Psychologie des Kindes*, Walter-Verlag, Olten, Switzerland, 1972.

128. Poggio, T., and Girosi, F., A theory of networks for approximation and learning, *MIT Artificial Intelligence Laboratory Memo 1140*, July 1989.

129. Reichardt, W., Umwandlung und Verarbeitung von Informationen im Zentralnervensystem und in Automaten, *Deutsche Medizinische Wochenschrift* **85** (23) (1960).

130. Reilly, D. L., Cooper, L. N., and Elbaum C., A neural model for category learning, *Biological Cybernetics* **45** (1982): 35–41.

131. Rexrodt, F. W., *Gehirn und Psyche*, Hippokrates Verlag, Stuttgart, Germany, 1981.

132. Ritter, H., and Schulten, K., On the stationary state of Kohonen's self-organizing sensory mapping, *Biological Cybernetics* **54** (1986): 1–8.

133. Ritter, H., Learning with the self-organizing map, in: *Proc. International Conference on Artificial Neural Networks*, Espoo, Finland, 1991, pp. 379–384.

134. Robbins, H., and Monro, S., A stochastic approximation method, *Annals of Mathematical Statistics* **22** (1951): 400–407.

135. Rolls, E. T., Principles underlying the representation and storage of information in neuronal networks in the primate hippocampus and cerebral cortex, in: Zornetzer, S. F., Davis, J. L., and Lau, C. (Eds.), *An Introduction to Neural and Electronic Networks*, Academic Press, New York, 1990, pp. 73–90.

136. Rosenblatt, F., *Principles of Neurodynamics*, Spartan Books, Washington, DC, 1961.

137. Rosenblatt, D., Lelu, A., and Georgel, A., Learning in a single pass: a neural model for principal component analysis and linear regression, in: *Proc. First IEE International Conference on Artificial Neural Networks*, London, 1989, pp. 252–256.

138. Ruck, D. W., et al., The multilayer perceptron as an approximation to a Bayes optimal discriminant function, *IEEE Transactions on Neural Networks* **1** (4) (1990): 296–298.

139. Rumelhart, D. E., Hinton, G. E., and Williams, R. J., Learning internal representation by error propagation, in: Rumelhart, D. E., and McClelland, J. L. (Eds.), *Parallel Distributed Processing*, Vol. 1, MIT Press, Cambridge, MA, 1986.

140. Rumelhart, D. E., and McClelland, J. L. (Eds.), *Parallel Distributed Processing*, Vol. 1, MIT Press, Cambridge, MA, 1986.

141. Rumelhart, D. E., and Zipser, D., Feature discovery by competitive learning, *Cognitive Science* **9** (1985): 75–112.

142. Schürmann, J., *Polynomklassifikatoren für die Zeichenerkennung*, Oldenbourg Verlag, Vienna, 1977.

143. von Seelen, W., and Mallot, H. A., Information processing in a neural architecture, in: *Proc. International Conference on Artificial Neural Networks*, Espoo, Finland, 1991, pp. 855–860.

144. von Seelen, W., and Mallot, H. A., Parallelism and redundancy in neural networks, in: Eckmiller, R., and von der Malsburg, C. (Eds.), *Neural Computers, NATO ASI Series F 41*, Springer-Verlag, Berlin, 1988, pp. 51–60.

145. Shastri, L., and Feldman, J. A., Evidential reasoning in semantic networks: a formal theory, in: *Proc. 9th International Joint Conference on Artificial Intelligence*, Los Angeles, 1985, pp. 465–474.

146. Shepanski, J. F., Fast learning in artificial neural systems: multilayer perceptron training using optimal estimation, in: *Proc. IEEE International Conference on Neural Networks*, Vol. 1, San Diego, CA, 1988, pp. 465–472.

147. Shepherd, G. M., *The Synaptic Organization of the Brain*, Oxford University Press, New York, 1974.

148. Shynk, J. J, Performance surfaces of a single-layer perceptron, *IEEE Transactions on Neural Networks* **1** (3) (1990): 268–274.

149. Sirat, J. A., Viala, J. R., and Remus, C., Image compression with competing multilayer perceptrons, in: *Proc. First IEE International Conference on Artificial Neural Networks*, London, 1989, pp. 404–408.

150. Smith, D. V., and Travers, J. B., A metric for the breadth of tuning of gustatory neurons, *Chemical Senses & Flavour* **4** (1979): 215–229.

151. Souček, B., and Souček, M., *Neural and Massively Parallel Computers*, Wiley, New York, 1988.

152. Spiegelhalter, D. J., Probabilistic reasoning in predictive expert systems, in: Kanal, L. N., and Lemmer, J. F. (Eds.), *Uncertainty in Artificial Intelligence*, North-Holland, Amsterdam, 1986, pp. 47–67.

153. Stepp, R. E., and Michalski, R. S., Conceptual clustering: inventing goal-oriented classifications of structured objects, in: Michalski, R. S., et al. (Eds.), *Machine Learning*, Vol. 2, Morgan Kaufmann, Los Altos, CA, 1986.

154. Tesauro, G., and Ahmad, S., Asymptotic convergence of backpropagation, *Neural Computation* **1** (1989): 382–391.

155. Uhr, L., Increasing the power of connectionist networks (CN) by improving structures, processes, learning, *Connection Science* **2** (3) (1990): 179–193.

156. Valiant, L. G., A theory of the learnable, *Communications of the ACM* **27** (11) (1984): 1134–1142.

157. Valiant, L. G., Learning disjunctions of conjunctions, in: *Proc. 9th International Joint Conference on Artificial Intelligence*, Los Angeles, 1985, pp. 560–566.

158. Vallbo, A. B., Muscle spindle responses at the onset of isometric voluntary contractions in man: time difference between fusimotor and skeletomotor effects, *Journal of Physiology* **218** (1971): 405–431.

159. Vapnik, V. N., and Chervonenkis, A. Ya., On the uniform convergence of relative frequencies of events to their probabilities, *Theory of Probability and Its Applications* **18** (1971): 264–280.

160. Vrckovnik, G., Carter, C. R., and Haykin, S., Radial basis function classification of impulse radar waveforms, in: *Proc. International Joint Conference on Neural Networks*, Vol. I, San Diego, CA, 1990, pp. 45–50.

161. Vrckovnik, G., Chung, T., and Carter, C. R., Classifying impulse radar waveforms using principal component analysis and neural networks, in: *Proc. International Joint Conference on Neural Networks*, Vol. I, San Diego, CA, 1990, pp. 69–74.

162. Walter, J. A., Martinetz, T. M., and Schulten, K. J., Industrial robot learns visuo-motor coordination by means of "neural-gas" network, in: *Proc. International Conference on Artificial Neural Networks*, Espoo, Finland, 1991, pp. 357–364.

163. Wan, E. A., Neural network classification: a Bayesian interpretation, *IEEE Transactions on Neural Networks* 1 (4) (1990): 303–305.

164. Wechsler, H., *Computational Vision*, Academic Press, New York, 1989.

165. Weiss, S. M., and Kapouleas, I., An empirical comparison of pattern recognition, neural nets, and machine learning classification methods, in: *Proc. 11th International Joint Conference on Artificial Intelligence*, Detroit, MI, 1989, pp. 781–787.

166. Werbos, P., Beyond regression: new techniques for prediction and analysis in the behavioral sciences, Ph.D. thesis, Harvard University, Cambridge, MA, November 1974.

167. Werbos, P., Backpropagation and neurocontrol: a review and prospectus, *Proc. International Joint Conference on Neural Networks*, Vol. 1, Washington, DC, 1989, pp. 209–216.

168. Widrow, B., An adaptive "Adaline" neuron using chemical "Memistors," *Technical Report 1553-2*, Stanford Electronics Laboratories, October 1960.

169. Widrow, B., and Smith, F. W., Pattern-recognizing control systems, in: *Computer and Information Sciences Symposium Proceedings*, Spartan Books, Washington, DC, 1963.

170. Widrow, G., and Hoff, M. E., Adaptive switching circuits, *Institute of Radio Engineers, Western Electronic Show and Convention, Convention Record*, Part 4, 1960, pp. 96–104.

INDEX